D1538431

PLAN TO WIN

PLAN TO WIN

A Definitive Guide to Business Processes

John Garside

Ichor Business Books
An Imprint of Purdue University Press
West Lafayette, Indiana

First Ichor Business Book edition, 1999.

Published under license from Macmillan Press Ltd., Houndsmills, Basingstoke, Hampshire RG21 6XS.

This edition available only in the United States and Canada.

03   02   01   00   99   1   2   3   4   5

Cover design by David Black.

ISBN 1-55753-163-3

Library of Congress Cataloging-in-Publication pending.

Printed in Great Britain

To my dear wife
Ros
for all her help and support in writing this book

Contents

Acknowledgements   xi

Introduction   xiii

1 Integrated Business Processes   **1**
Introduction to Business Processes   3
Organisation Structure   4
People   6
Strategy Development   11
Information Technology   15

2 Key Elements of a Business Plan   **21**
The Introduction   23
Business Development and Sales   25
Product Introduction   32
Supply-chain Management   36
Distribution and Aftermarket   44
Business Support   46
Customer Satisfaction and Quality   47
Programme Management   49
Financial Management and Control   50
Business Strategy and Actions   55

3 Customer Development Process   **59**
Introduction   61
Market Overview   61
Market Forecast   62
Business Intelligence System   63
Opportunity Evaluation   65
Identify the Opportunity   66
Evaluation of Requirements   69
Product and Project Approval   75
Bid Preparation   84
Winning the Contract   90
Summary   92

4 Product Introduction Process **95**
Introduction 97
Technology Route Map 97
Product Introduction Plan 100
Product Introduction Resources 102
Project Classification 104
A Generic Product Introduction Process 105
Product and Process Design 111
Concept Validation 118
Process Implementation 123
Manufacturing Support 130
Project Management 134
Summary 136

5 Supply-chain Management **137**
Overview 139
Strategic Sourcing 140
Factory Space and Location 141
Manufacturing Systems and Equipment 145
Assembly and Test Activities 149
Machining Facilities 149
Internal Factory Capacity 150
Production Planning and Control 156
Measures of Performance 156
Organisation 160
Quality Systems 161
Human Resources 162
New Product Introduction Process 166
Summary 166

6 Industrial Distribution Management **169**
Introduction 171
Strategic Analysis 171
Market Flowout 172
Key Buying Factors by Market Segment 174
Customer Trends and Forecasting 176
Strategic Local Market Planning 180
Competitor Profile 182
Market Attractiveness 182
SWOT Analysis 183

Positioning the Branch 184
Tactical Sales Techniques 186
Customer Selection 187
Sales Planning 188
Sales Action Processes 190
Selling Techniques 191
Sales-force Effectiveness 193
Evaluation and Appraisal 194
Measures of Performance 195
Summary 197

7 Customer Satisfaction and Quality **199**
Introduction 201
Establishing Customer Monitors and Reporting Systems 201
Customer Satisfaction Route Map 204
Creating and Communicating the Vision 204
Code of Ethical Conduct 207
Customer-focused programmes 208
The Quality-improvement Process 211
Safety Review Board 213
Formal Quality Procedures 214
Statistical Methods and Process Control 216
Quality-improvement Route Maps 219
Performance Measures 224
Summary 224

8 Project Management **225**
Introduction 227
The Change Process 227
Project Management 230
Formal Project Management Procedures 232
Resource-planning and Cost-estimating 237
Project Control 239
Project Reporting 241
Risk Management 245
Hazard Reports 246
Change Control 248
The Role of the Project Manager 250
Summary 252

9 Finance Management   **255**
    Introduction   257
    Financial Reporting   257
    Forecasting Results   262
    Financial Control   262
    Costing Systems   263
    Non-financial Measures of Performance   264
    Business Awareness and Understanding   267
    Investment Sanctions   269
    Capital Sanctions   272
    Summary   274

Conclusion   **276**

References and Supporting Literature   277

Index   279

Acknowledgements

Over the years, I have been privileged to work with many talented people in a variety of companies including Dunlop, GKN and Lucas. My involvement with a broad spectrum of managers has had a significant impact upon my thinking, stimulating the development of many ideas and concepts needed for implementing successful business processes described here in my book.

My thanks go to all these people, and in particular:

Frank Turner for initiating my understanding of business process engineering and the concept of customer satisfaction and quality management.

Professor John Parnaby for giving me experience and his knowledge of manufacturing systems, supply-chain strategy and project management.

Ken Maciver for introducing me to the necessity for rigorous application of procedures needed for effective business and financial planning.

Jack Fryer for outlining the structure of a robust product introduction process.

David Bundred for initiating the concepts needed for promoting industrial distribution and sales.

I would also like to thank Professor Kumar Bhattacharyya and the Warwick International Manufacturing Group for giving me the opportunity and facilities needed to compile this book.

JOHN GARSIDE

Introduction

This book was written to capture and pass on the benefit of my knowledge gained from 25 years experience working in the highly competitive Industrial, Automotive and Aerospace international component supply industries, for companies including Plessey, Sperry Vickers, Dunlop, GKN and Lucas. It is written for managers, both senior and junior, who are expected to develop key aspects of the company business plan, and are challenged with identifying and implementing cost-effective business processes.

The book focuses on the key elements of a robust business plan, defining the core business processes needed in a successful process-driven organisation. The core processes have been described to embrace all the necessary activities, supported by diagrams and checklists of the critical items that must be considered when designing the process. An experienced manager could use the process descriptions and checklists to make critical assessments against current practice, to confirm '*We do that! That's not relevant to us! How did we miss . . .?*' In my experience, most major problems arise from those items that were initially missed by the management team.

At the business process concept level, considerable similarities exist in the core processes required to manage businesses. The differences are dependent upon the type of business and actual tasks being performed. For instance, no standard recipe exists for making a cake, but mixing a number of different basic ingredients and cooking them in an oven is a common process and the type of cake produced varies depending upon its particular use.

The concepts are based upon personal experience of working in different industries, having to resolve difficult business issues, and finding solutions to complex technical problems in factories around the world. However, the most important aspect has been my association with many excellent senior managers and colleagues with whom I have worked. All the information is founded on practical aspects of work undertaken throughout my career, and many principles have been implemented in several businesses and sectors of industry across the world. Once its content has been broadly understood, the book may be used as a common reference, confirming that those items important to creating a successful business are fully considered, and all appropriate actions taken.

I am Principal Fellow at Warwick International Manufacturing Group, having joined in 1997 after an industrial career which included appointments as Programme Director (Lucas Aerospace), Development Director (Lucas Fluid Power, at the time the largest Fluid Power Distributor in the World), Group Manufacturing Systems Engineer (Lucas CAV), Head of Manufacturing Systems Division (GKN Technology), Manager Manufacturing Engineering (Dunlop Technology), and Technical Manager (Dunlop Hose Division). I hope that this book will become the best available industrial guide to business processes.

1

Integrated Business Processes

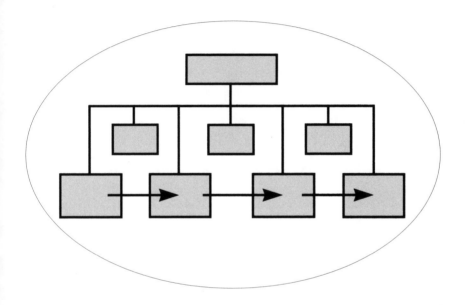

Topics

Introduction to business processes
Organisation structure
People
Strategy development
Information technology

1

Integrated Business Processes

INTRODUCTION TO BUSINESS PROCESSES

Businesses have been traditionally structured around functional organisations that evolved from the principles promoted by Adam Smith two hundred years ago. His concepts were based upon dividing the manufacturing process into a number of simple tasks, and these principles became entrenched in our Western manufacturing practices.

The shop-floor environment was transformed by the advent of the Japanese manufacturing philosophy, which involved people accepting the need to design the process and take responsibility for a number of tasks, working in teams to operate and continually improve the process. The Japanese focused upon eliminating the non-value added activities while ensuring that all processes were capable, consistently making products to very high quality standards. Many companies have learnt from their experience and the Western world now has some excellent examples of effective manufacturing systems. The revolution of the manufacturing environment should now be extended to encompass broader business activities. This will only occur once the concepts of organising the business around key business processes have been assimilated by the senior management team responsible for the organisational structure.

To make the transition it is important to understand the concept of a business process. A process could be expressed as:

A number of interrelated activities needed to accomplish a specific task

The overall objective for most businesses is to sustain a viable operation through generating *profit* and *cash* to meet all stakeholders' expectations. In manufacturing-based companies, this is usually achieved through establishing plans with management organisations responsible for the following business activities:

3

- Identifying customer needs and winning orders;
- Introducing innovative products, enhancing existing designs and developing manufacturing processes to exceed the customer's expectation;
- Procuring materials, manufacturing and assembling components to meet agreed customer delivery schedules;
- Establishing a distribution network and supporting the product in service.

The relative importance of each area varies with the type of business and particular market sectors being served, but some combination of these activities exists within most businesses.

Activities that address the key business requirements, comprise the core elements of the business process

Consequently, the generic business processes may be defined as:

- Business Development and Sales
- Product Introduction Management
- Supply Chain Management
- Distribution and Aftermarket Support

The way these processes operate depends upon the industrial sector and structure of the company. However, creating an organisation around *key business processes* removes the departmental barriers found in traditional businesses and provides a foundation for building a team-based organisation with clear ownership for meeting committed business and financial objectives.

ORGANISATION STRUCTURE

Management and organisation govern how a business operates, therefore it is essential to have an appropriate management structure that provides ownership for each business process and a method for managing the interfaces between them. In its simplest form, an organisation needs a general manager and an owner for each key business process:

- Business development and sales manager
- Product introduction manager
- Supply-chain manager
- Distribution and aftermarket manager

In larger or more complex companies, the five operational roles above need support from three staff activities that operate in a matrix mode across the business processes. These roles are:

1. *Customer satisfaction and quality manager* – represents the customer within the management team, having authority to ensure products meet all quality standards and exceed customer expectation.
2. *Programme manager* – responsible for ensuring that *changes* are implemented, and new products introduced within agreed costs and time scales, using the disciplines of good project management.
3. *Finance manager* – ensures that financial accounts are professionally managed, and profit and cash commitments are delivered, through controlling expenditures within agreed budgets.

In practice, more than one activity may be owned by the same person if individual owners cannot be justified due to the size of the job. However, if a manager is not assigned to a process, then responsibility for the role reverts to the general manager.

Therefore, a possible management structure for a process based organisation could be that shown in Figure 1.1. The need for a dedicated manager for each process is governed by the type of business, size of job, its level within the company and the strategy being pursued. The organisation chart in Figure 1.2 illustrates a reporting structure that may exist at different levels within a large company. A business may choose to combine areas of responsibility, managing the process at the most appropriate level. However, it is essential to ensure that a recognised reporting structure is established and all activities are covered in the design and definition of people's job roles.

The job roles require further definition, but the structures illustrate a possible framework for a business operating with a full spectrum of business processes and organised at different levels around a number of defined business groupings within the overall company.

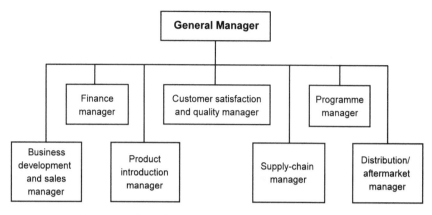

Figure 1.1   Management structure

The other traditional management staff activities – personnel and information technology – may also be introduced to strengthen a management team, depending upon the business needs. These roles are important but are not directly involved in managing the key business processes, and with the increasing trend for outsourcing of non-core services, specialists may be brought in to support management teams when the need arises.

PEOPLE

People are the most valuable asset in a business because they have the knowledge, the commitment and the determination to succeed. Working in teams, people can achieve much more than as individuals. Therefore, it is incumbent upon management to appoint a business team and create a working environment capable of winning (Figure 1.3). In my opinion, introducing integrated business processes is fundamental to creating competitive advantage by simplifying the overall management process. The traditional underlying principle of people performing discrete simple tasks has resulted in complex business control systems that are virtually impossible to manage. The way forward demands teams of people who perform a number of interrelated tasks that make the overall processes easier to manage. This is dependent upon skills being embedded in the workforce, with everyone accepting the challenge of continual personal development. The current workforce will comprise the majority of people employed

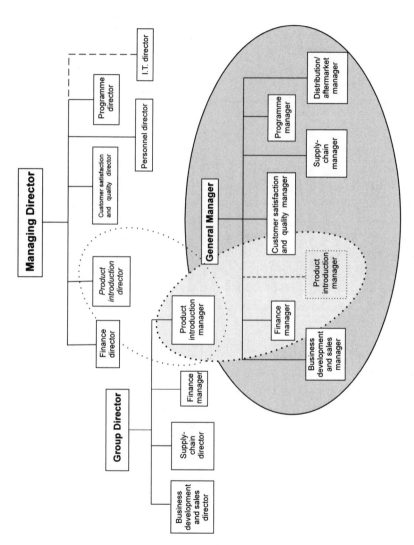

Figure 1.2 Organisation structure

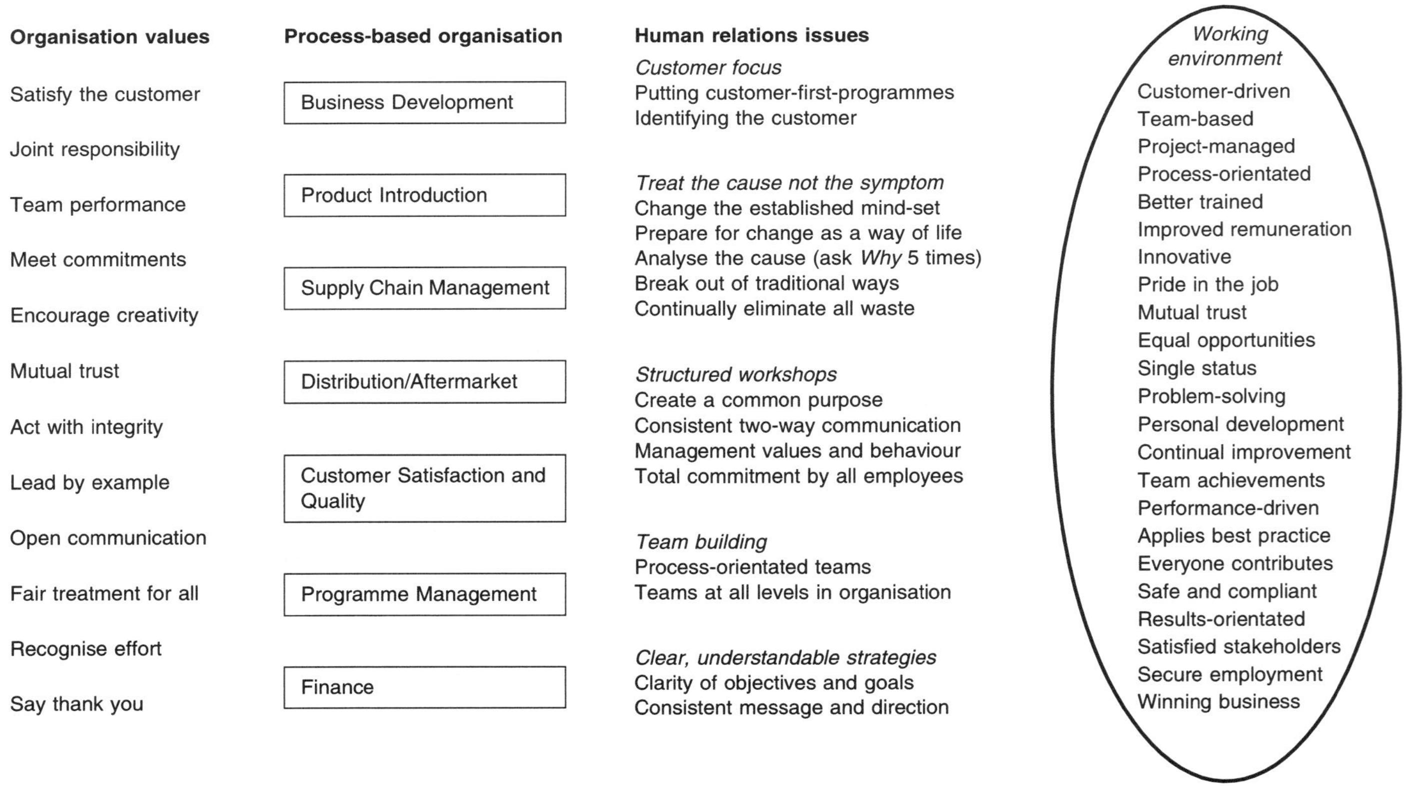

Organisation values

Satisfy the customer

Joint responsibility

Team performance

Meet commitments

Encourage creativity

Mutual trust

Act with integrity

Lead by example

Open communication

Fair treatment for all

Recognise effort

Say thank you

Process-based organisation

Business Development

Product Introduction

Supply Chain Management

Distribution/Aftermarket

Customer Satisfaction and Quality

Programme Management

Finance

Human relations issues

Customer focus
Putting customer-first-programmes
Identifying the customer

Treat the cause not the symptom
Change the established mind-set
Prepare for change as a way of life
Analyse the cause (ask *Why* 5 times)
Break out of traditional ways
Continually eliminate all waste

Structured workshops
Create a common purpose
Consistent two-way communication
Management values and behaviour
Total commitment by all employees

Team building
Process-orientated teams
Teams at all levels in organisation

Clear, understandable strategies
Clarity of objectives and goals
Consistent message and direction

Working environment

Customer-driven
Team-based
Project-managed
Process-orientated
Better trained
Improved remuneration
Innovative
Pride in the job
Mutual trust
Equal opportunities
Single status
Problem-solving
Personal development
Continual improvement
Team achievements
Performance-driven
Applies best practice
Everyone contributes
Safe and compliant
Results-orientated
Satisfied stakeholders
Secure employment
Winning business

Figure 1.3 The working environment

in ten years time, therefore the way forward is to establish an Employee Development Route Map that guides people through the transition, establishing a working environment where people want to work and be part of a successful team. The route map is not a panacea, but provides the direction in which a company must be prepared to travel.

A company where people are proud to work as a team and gain job satisfaction, must ultimately be more successful than one driven by fear and rhetoric

Making the transition is probably the most difficult, but also the most rewarding management task. The changes must include everyone in the organisation demanding greater changes of management thinking than subordinates. It will take several years to accomplish, with people gaining confidence and mutual trust, demonstrated through delighting customers and delivering financial commitments to shareholders.

Employee Framework

Introducing new working practices has to be supported by a framework that identifies the characteristics of the desired working environment. This requires:

- No false barriers to achieving full job flexibility, except a person's own ability;
- Everyone having the same basic terms and conditions of employment as allowed by national legislation;
- Appropriate training being available to advance knowledge and skills;
- Remuneration systems rewarding the acquisition and application of skills;
- People being encouraged to achieve their full potential;
- Recognising people giving leadership and accepting responsibility;
- A working environment founded upon mutual respect and trust;
- People feeling involved, committed, and seeking opportunities for improvement;
- Teams accepting ownership and responsibility for delivering tasks on time.

Establishing this framework and upholding the organisation values is extremely demanding upon management resolve. However, once a workforce has been convinced, and existing traditional working practices are being overhauled to introduce new ways of working, management must *never* contemplate taking advantage of the situation for short-term gain. This would irrevocably damage the mutual trust, destroying the climate needed for long term change and ultimate survival.

Communication

Good management communication is essential if the workforce is to accept management plans that must be implemented to improve or restore profitability. The workforce may have to bear the consequences of difficult management decisions such as:

- Redundancies;
- Site integration and restructuring;
- Call for total dedication to resolve product performance problems;
- Need for absolute adherence to procedure to recover persistent quality problems;
- Recover hostile customer relationships;
- Acceptance of *more* best practices.

In these situations it is vitally important for management to retain the trust and confidence of the workforce, particularly when the future is uncertain. This can only be achieved through well-structured formal and informal communication, using every available medium to provide accurate information, and dispel the rumours that inevitably circulate.

Employee Development

The rate of any change is ultimately dictated by the skill of the workforce. Business processes can be designed, new plant and equipment purchased, but if the workforce lacks the skills or has not been trained to work the new systems, then improvement goals will never be realised. The employee development task is company-wide, as people are required to obtain a wider range of skills, crossing traditional educational boundaries.

Examples of the *broader management skills* needed by a process-driven organisation are:

- *Customer satisfaction and quality manager* – needs the skill and experience to gain credibility with customers and has the knowledge to implement integrated quality procedures for product and process improvement.
- *Product introduction manager* – needs to understand both the product technology and advanced manufacturing processes to develop high quality cost-effective products.
- *Supply-chain manager* – takes full responsibility for the site, agreeing the customer schedule, procuring components and delivering quality products on time to the customer.

The need to define and introduce broader job roles applies to most jobs within a simplified process-based organisation. This places greater importance upon structured career development and succession planning. People with the necessary range of skills are not readily available from the existing traditional job market, therefore it is incumbent upon the management team to take responsibility for ensuring that people with the required abilities are trained and given the opportunity to demonstrate their full potential. The challenge of providing this broader-based training is fully accepted by the Warwick International Manufacturing Group at Warwick University. All postgraduate training is undertaken in collaboration with companies, and provides people with the full range of skills needed to operate in a process-based organisation, capable of competing effectively in global markets.

STRATEGY DEVELOPMENT

The business strategy must be developed as an interactive activity, based upon the information and analysis undertaken when preparing the business plan. It is an integral process, stepping back from the 'detail' and makes an informed, realistic assessment of the opportunities and future direction for the business. The company vision, competitor analysis, assessment of external drivers and the business financial objectives are reviewed in relation to the customer base and the features that make customers select particular suppliers.

These are closely examined to determine:

- *Competencies* that must be retained and developed by the business;
- Core *technologies* embodied in the product and process that must be retained to protect the business and retain proprietary knowledge;
- Activities and areas where the business should *focus resources* to develop the product range and exploit market opportunities;
- Management *values* and *behaviour* that will be adopted to create a stable environment with a motivated and highly skilled workforce;
- The *resource* and *investments* required to compete effectively in chosen markets.

Critical factors that are key to becoming a world-class supplier, capable of generating a superior financial performance, must be identified. These are then compared to the present business performance to establish *gaps* in performance, identifying strategic options and operational business objectives (Figure 1.4).

The essence of strategic development is examining *external events* that are influencing the business and its markets. It is important to identify competitor actions and possible strategies at the earliest opportunity, developing tactics for rebuffing possible assaults aimed at enticing away present customers. There is no substitute for robust internal plans but these will not always identify the entrepreneurial opportunities that arise as markets mature and new territories become available for increasing sales. These will only transpire through critically examining the industry and relentlessly exploring all possibilities for developing new business.

Features that should be considered in performing a strategic analysis include:

- The position of the business in the industry, examining its size relative to other companies and its ability to compete.
- Relationship with competitors.
- Methods of securing business.
- Activities across the industry, examining long-term trends and capacity available.
- Global demand and reasons for expansion or consolidation within different territories.
- Actions being taken by competitors to secure commercial advantage.

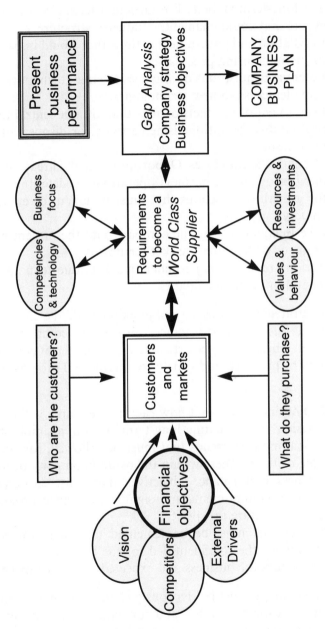

Figure 1.4 Business strategy

- Credible 'change the game' strategies that could revolutionise the industry.
- The long-term viability for particular technologies and foreseeable events that could change the industry structure.
- Legislation and government actions that would impact the product or manufacturing processes.
- Potential acquisitions or alliances to strengthen market position or provide access to new technologies.
- Divestment of products or sites that are not central to longer-term profitability, by rationalising capacity, or disposal of loss-making operations.
- Strengths, Weaknesses, Opportunities and Threats analysis, examining in detail the business operations to determine the potential for growth, and actions that must be taken to retain stakeholder value.
- Investments made by the company and the present market leader in major or potential market territories.
- Actions required in particular markets due to political, environmental or economic factors.

This strategic analysis, in conjunction with the business plan and present business performance, allows the company strategy and business objectives to be articulated. A number of concise statements should be prepared and widely communicated providing information on:

- The business aims and how each process area will operate.
- A vision, encapsulating long-term goals in a simple statement.
- Global industry trends that must be followed, for success.
- Role of the business within the overall company portfolio.
- Business performance objectives that must delivered, including financial commitments and significant change projects necessary to ensure future prosperity.
- Policies that must be implemented to sustain the business, and accomplish the role identified for the business.
- Key values for business and expected standards of behaviour.

The strategy must be rigorously challenged by the senior management team for its validity and robustness prior to implementation. However, once agreed, it must remain consistent and time allowed to deliver the expected benefits. The overall direction must be reviewed regularly, but this should only result in tactical changes to achieve particular milestones, not a reversal in basic principles. Developing a sound strategy is fundamental to business survival, but it must be understood that once actions have been initiated they can be extremely difficult to reverse.

INFORMATION TECHNOLOGY

Information technology is currently the most powerful tool available for improving the effectiveness of people employed in the business. The pace of change in information technology is formidable – any system purchased will be superseded by a new one within a year. These relentless improvements cannot be used as a reason for not investing, because information technology is a catalyst for designing effective business processes. The ability to share information and use common databases is revolutionising the concepts that can be applied to the design of specific business processes. However, two facts remain consistent:

1. information technology is a *tool* used to *support* the business process; and
2. the *information system* and *organisation structure* are dependent upon the same information flow and are, therefore, closely related.

The challenge is to introduce cost-effective integrated systems based upon standard hardware and software, with all elements of information being assigned an owner who is responsible for the accuracy of the data residing in a single database location. The elements of a standard system are as shown in Figure 1.5.

Software packages have been developed for most processes as stand-alone solutions. The challenge is to establish an integrated suite of programmes that allow several users to work from the same database, but have the information structured to meet specific requirements of the person performing the task. When designing business systems and selecting support tools, it must be remembered that *processes may need to be performed using more than one method.* These differing requirements must be analysed to determine the most appropriate way of undertaking the task, if necessary using alternative systems for supporting the process. For example, the product introduction process may require three-dimensional solid models for constructing complex surfaces, but these systems can be linked to less

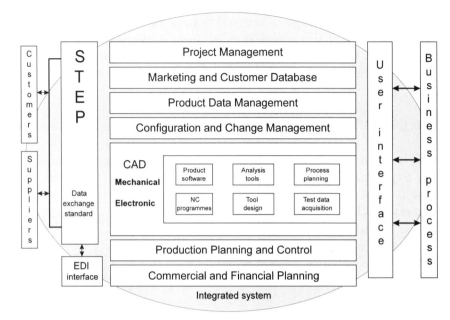

Figure 1.5   Elements of an IT system

sophisticated drafting packages to support more 'routine' aspects of the product introduction design process. The main reason, in my experience, for IT systems failing to deliver the promised benefits, is that vendors sell all-embracing and over-complicated solutions designed to handle all the requirements using the same method. This generally means the system is over sophisticated for 80 per cent of the tasks, but incapable of performing the remaining 20 per cent. Early generation manufacturing resource planning systems in the 1980s clearly demonstrated these characteristics.

Elements of the business process benefiting from information technology support tools are:

- **Project management** – a variety of software packages are available for planning and controlling different types of project. They are useful for generating a critical path for events, identifying milestones, estimating resources and monitoring progress. However, project management systems are not, at present, integrated into the overall business control system.
- **Marketing and customer database** – general packages are available, but companies have often developed bespoke systems capturing

information relevant to particular customer groups. General PC-based systems using standard integrated business packages are becoming increasingly popular. These are used to structure customer notes by gathering information from visits reports, press articles and expert comment and opinion. Information is obtained using electronic mail or scanned directly from published articles; it is then collated in standard format and circulated using electronic mail.

- **Product data management** – systems are being applied to provide a common repository for associated product, process and quality data. PDM allows ready access to relevant information aimed at reducing:

  - product introduction lead-times,
  - product cost-structures, and
  - non-recurring product and process development expenses.

- **Configuration and change management** – these systems are the foundation of rigorous product introduction management. Customers are demanding greater product variety, sometimes crafted to individual requirements. They control product change requests, ensuring that modifications are embodied within the current configuration release and full traceability records are maintained.

- **Computer aided design** – product design systems are migrating towards three-dimensional solid modelling, as the tools offered by a number of leading vendors become more cost-effective. Particular systems are suited to different applications, with a clear distinction between mechanical and electronic design systems. The task is to integrate the various tools needed to create a comprehensive data pack that confirms the product's conformance to specification, providing a definition for the manufacturing and quality processes. The tools that need to be integrated include:

  - software that defines the product's parametric geometry ensuring fit, form and function;
  - analytical tools capable of generating representative mathematical models of the product's dynamic performance under a variety of operating conditions;
  - process-planning systems based upon the geometric model. Parameters are translated into specific manufacturing requirements, providing a production layout and associated quality and work instructions;

- numerical control programming of machine tools. These should be capable of being downloaded directly onto the machine, generating the cutter paths or controlling operating parameters needed to manufacture the product;
- post-processors that translate the cutter path data into machine code for a particular NC control system;
- drafting systems to support the design of fixtures and tooling needed to hold and process material passing through the manufacturing operations;
- test data acquisition for taking test rig information, correlating it directly with mathematical models to determine an optimum solution;
- knowledge-based systems that capture procedures, reducing the time taken for further iterations of more lengthy procedures;
- process modelling using discrete event simulation to optimise the process and flow of materials; and
- manufacturing system design tools for developing manufacturing facilities appropriate to the business and market requirements.

- **Production planning and control** – several vendors have comprehensive integrated packages aimed at controlling manufacturing activities. Links needed into other business systems have usually been defined, and if the system is compatible and applied without significant modification it can be very effective. However, the fundamental management requirements for implementing a successful manufacturing control system are:

  - data in the system must have an accuracy level greater than 98 per cent;
  - the system is simplified whenever possible; for example by taking a large number of low-value items off the automated planning system and setting up a re-order procedure based upon usage;
  - use the planning information and work in accordance with the system;
  - establish single databases with identified owners for critical information – bills of materials, process routings, customer order files and so on;
  - implement master production planning at three levels:

    (1) master production schedule owned by the general manager for determining the long-term capacity requirements;

(2) production schedule for ensuring materials and components will be available in time to fulfill the production plan; and

(3) production plan stating the manufacturing commitment over the reporting period.

- adopt more than one method for planning and controlling in-process materials;
- use actual process routes, machining times and changeover times in the production-planning system;
- identify and control bottlenecks in the supply-chain process;
- confirm the production plan is achievable within available capacity; and
- make factory planning a senior management task. Optimising the large number of variables requires intelligent thinking and intimate process knowledge.

- **Commercial and financial planning** – many software packages are available to support this. They offer an integrated solution for a number of standard business transactions, but have to be adopted and applied as a complete system. Again, they are most effective when implemented without significant modifications. However, they focus upon specific financial measures and these often require broader definitions to incorporate other important non-financial parameters needed to assess the performance of the business, a supplier or the perceptions of a customer.

- **Customer satisfaction and quality systems** – tend to be a collection of individual packages that address specific requirements:

  - database for monitoring and tracking in-service product quality;
  - customer information and record of quality delivery and cost;
  - costs associated with quality; and
  - service incidents and corrective actions reports.

- **Customer service systems** – comprise a number of specialist IT systems and packages for producing customer service information needed for:

  - product literature;
  - technical publications;
  - service manuals and bulletins; and
  - instruction and installation documents.

- **Personnel systems** – these tend to be specialist packages but the information is crucial to the future of the business, being a basis for career development and planning.

- **PC-based word processing, spreadsheet, and presentation packages** – these IT tools have become a key element of everyday business practice. It is incumbent upon everyone in the organisation, irrespective of age or status, to exploit the benefits gained through applying these fundamental tools. Systems become easier to use with each release of software and PC upgrade. They have the potential to inspire and support new business process concepts, removing layers and limits imposed by a traditional 'wiring diagram'-type organisation

Networks and Communications

Communicating between different vendors' systems is a limitation for information technology providers. Compatibility can be achieved using electronic data interface standards, allowing information created in different formats to be translated and displayed on a variety of platforms. This works well for text and two-dimensional drawings, but significant problems arise when attempting to transfer three-dimensional solid model information between different vendors' systems. An international data exchange standard (STEP) has been agreed between vendors and major customers, and considerable progress has been made towards translating objects, but these currently lose connectivity that allows the model to be used for engineering analysis.

The use of electronic mailing systems has become an accepted method of sending and receiving information. The ability to exchange documents and drawings over the network and receive *original* quality copies provides another valuable tool that allows procedures needed for effective business processes to be redefined. The potential of this technology should be exploited and it is the responsibility of everyone in the organisation to use these tools in innovative ways, taking full advantage of commercial and cost-saving opportunities. The use of video-conferencing will facilitate national and international meetings without the need for regular, time-consuming travel. The Internet will expand its role as a provider of information and support services.

Information technology is still in its infancy and has the greatest potential of any new technology to revolutionise the operation of a company. However, it must be applied intelligently in a business system designed to innovate and change ways of working.

2

Key Elements of a Business Plan

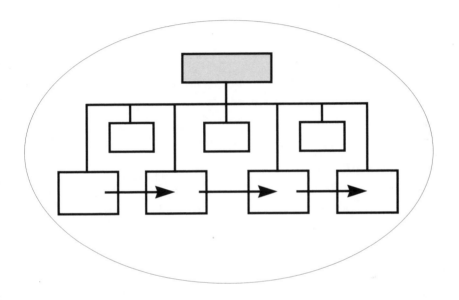

Topics

The introduction
Business development and sales
Product introduction
Supply-chain management
Distribution and aftermarket
Business support
Customer satisfaction and quality
Programme management
Financial management and control
Business strategy and actions

2

Key Elements of a Business Plan

The company business plan is the most important document a management team prepares because it sets the future direction and financial commitments for the plan period (usually three or five years). Business plans have traditionally been prepared from a collection of departmental plans and collated into one overall plan. This approach suffers from the same deficiencies found in functional organisations, and therefore a business must instigate a business planning process around the fundamental processes which drive it.

It is also the formal document that sells the business potential to directors and external advisors. The purpose of the plan is to allow people who are not directly involved in day-to-day activities to assimilate the important features of the business and provide the necessary financial support needed to implement the proposals. Business plans should be well presented, concise, precise and understandable. They must be structured and tailored to a particular company's requirements, but a good business plan should address the following aspects:

THE INTRODUCTION

The introduction provides a two-page executive summary of the business and its position within the industry, addressing:

- Present market and expected trends;
- Outline of the business position in the market;
- Major issues that have been identified in the business plan; and
- Summary of actions needed to achieve the financial commitments.

It should also provide a number of lists and charts, such as Tables 2.1 and 2.2, permitting people not closely associated with the business,

Table 2.1 *Characteristics of market*

Strong growth in civil markets	Dominated by US industry
Recovery in aftermarket demand	Captive aftermarket
Controlled by six key suppliers	Strong barriers to entry
Market has over-capacity	Weaker companies will not survive

Table 2.2 *Business strengths and weaknesses*

Strengths	*Weaknesses*
Good market position	High manufacturing cost structure
Strong technology	Engineering not customer-focused
International presence	Functional organisation
Broad product base	

but critical to agreeing the plan, to quickly assimilate the key issues facing the business and the significant features related to the products.

Summary of Business Objectives

- Achieve world-class cost and asset performance;
- Delight customers through exceeding expectations;
- Achieve product technology leadership;
- Organise the business around key business processes;
- Strengthen the presence in the Asia Pacific regions.

Lists and charts should also be presented summarising the following key attributes:

- Strategic role of the business within the company;
- Strategy and goals;
- Challenges facing the business in the short, medium and long term;
- Key actions needed to deliver the plan;
- Summary of the market position by major segment:
  - ○ size of market,
  - ○ market share,
  - ○ market segmentation, and
  - ○ position relative to major competition.

- Summary of the key financial commitments:

  o sales,
  o trading profit,
  o profit before interest and tax,
  o operating cash flow,
  o capital expenditure, and
  o product introduction costs.

- Summary of key ratios:

  o return on sales,
  o return on capital employed,
  o capital turnover ratio,
  o sales per employee, and
  o added value per employee.

- Statement of critical non-financial measures:

  o number of employees,
  o quality index, and
  o stock turns.

BUSINESS DEVELOPMENT AND SALES

Market Overview and Sales Plan

The overall market is examined in a global context, and in relationship to the major segments that are important to the business. This section should review the range of products within the business portfolio, establishing the level of *sales, gross margin and profit* expected by major product lines over the period of the plan, providing commentary on critical features that will impact potential sales:

- Major market segments;
- Prime factors that drive the market;
- Impact on market through growth in gross domestic product.
- Influence of an ageing population in industrial countries;
- Movement in specific market segments;
- Specific events that will impact the market;
- New legislation and social trends;
- Impact of new technology;
- Influence of other elements in the value chain;
- Movement in exchange rates and monetary policy.

Exhibits should be presented showing an overview of the overall market, with numerical information on the past year's performance, the current forecast, and projections for future years. For example, the Aircraft industry would possibly consider the factors shown in Table 2.3.

Information presented should include aspects relevant to a particular business and may include the following:

- Movement in the economy, global and major markets;
- Predicted growth in overall product or service demand;
- Related economic factors that influence market (for example, new building starts, increased wage rates, increased car sales, expected aircraft orders);
- National events that impact the market;
- Impact from new legislation;
- Privatisation of industry;
- New technology that will change the market;
- Mergers and industrial consolidation.

Market Segmentation and Projected Trends

A statement is required defining the key market segments that comprise the business, together with graphical information that illustrates the relative size and growth of each element within the segment. As an example for the aircraft industry, the information would illustrate demand for the different types of aircraft, as shown in Figure 2.1.

This section should close with a summary of the impact these factors will have on the business performance, and a statement of how they will be addressed by the business team.

Current and Projected Market Share

This section compares the business with its competitors, particularly in relation to products with a good market position and those with growth potential. It should also review the overall product portfolio to establish which products generate the majority of the sales and profit within the markets segments they serve. A statement on the market position is required for each significant market sector, with a projection of future demand and corresponding business potential.

Table 2.3 *Typical aerospace industry statistics*

		1995	1996	1997	1998	1999	2000	2001	2002	2003
Economy (real GDP)	World	1.60%	1.30%	2.80%	3.00%	2.50%	2.80%	2.80%	3.00%	3.00%
	USA	2.60%	3.00%	4.10%	3.30%	2.50%	2.20%	2.00%	2.50%	2.50%
Airline traffic	World	9.40%	3.40%	7.90%	6.00%	5.40%	5.00%	4.80%	4.80%	4.70%
	USA	6.50%	2.20%	6.20%	3.00%	4.20%	4.00%	3.00%	3.50%	3.50%
Airline earnings OP profits	World	$1.0 bn	$2.5 bn	$8.0 bn	$11.0 bn	$15.0 bn	$15.0 bn	$10.0 bn	$8.0 bn	$8.0 bn
	USA	$2.2 bn	$1.0 bn	$2.1 bn	$4.5 bn	$6.0 bn	$6.0 bn	$4.5 bn	$3.5 bn	$4.0 bn
Aircraft orders		469	406	350	715	600	600	600	500	500
Aircraft deliveries		785	650	517	487	500	576	606	621	631
Stored aircraft		1003	1089	933	680	540	500	400	300	350
Retirements		134	118	210	217	237	300	300	280	270

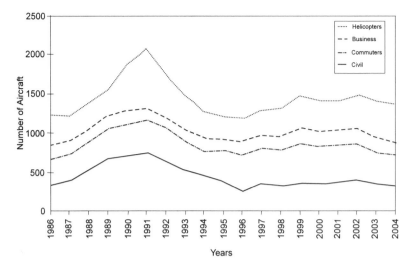

Figure 2.1   Estimated cumulative aircraft demand

Information on market share can be presented in several ways, but the most common format is to provide pie charts for the various market sectors showing the current position and at the end of the planning period (see Figure 2.2). The size of the segment shows the relative size of major competitors and the diameter of the pie can be used to show the size of the market in different years.

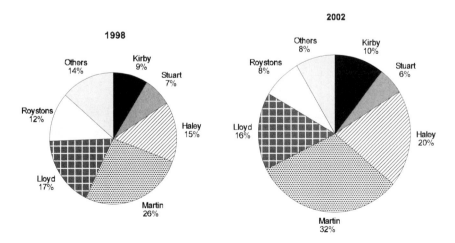

Figure 2.2   Current and projected market share

Additional Marketing Information that may be Included if Relevant to the Business Strategy

Product Group Market Growth

This information can be illustrated by a series of stack charts that show the growth or decline in a market segment, and the share of the market that is held by the major competitors with respect to key time periods. The factors that are driving the change in the market should be explained.

Key Industry Trends

Analysis of industry trends and factors driving change in the marketplace. This requires considerable research to understand the underlying issues changing the industry. Many factors have to be reviewed and ranked in order of priority to establish the critical business drivers.

Technology Trends

These can be plotted on a matrix showing market attractiveness (high, medium, low) versus competitive position (weak, average, strong). Circles are drawn showing the size of the potential market with a pie-slice representing the share achieved by the business. An arrow then shows the direction of the technology due to the changing customer need and alternative products.

Customer Characteristics

This section analyses the customer base and characterises it by type, prime manufacturers, aftermarket customers, governments, or other manufacturers in the value chain. The business will require different strategies for generating sales in each of these markets, therefore a statement is required on the main reasons for sales. Sales to an original equipment manufacturer will be based upon achieving preferred supplier status, but it is important to analyse the primary and secondary qualifying requirements for obtaining sales with particular types of customer.

Table 2.4   *Customer characteristics*

Prime OEM	Position	Sales	Importance to the company
Aircar	Dominant in large transport, strategy to dominate the market	£30m	Opportunity to provide valves on new large transport
Abbey	Joint venture with Martin to form the largest systems supplier	£48m	Follow on business and opportunity to gain access to Martin products
JJ	Won major contract for up-rated engine on new large aircraft	£32m	Provide entry into US airlines

Governments	Position	Sales	Importance to the company
MOD	Specifies the military requirements for the UK	£57m	Provides the opportunity to obtain work on the next generation of military aircraft and purchases spares
DOD	Specifies the military requirements for the USA	£47m	Provides entry onto the JSE programme

End-users	Position	Sales	Importance to the company
BB	Largest US carrier	£3m	Provides contact with significant end user and purchases high value spares

The reasons for obtaining sales varies considerably, and while *initial cost* is always a factor, many other items have considerable influence:

- Total cost of ownership;
- On-time delivery;
- Legal requirements;
- Place of manufacture.

This can be supported using a chart as shown in Table 2.4. This contains information on the primary customers, their position in the market and relative size, sales value to the business and a brief description of how important individual customers are to the business.

Competitor Profiles

Another aspect that must be considered is the competitor base. Major competitors have to be systematically analysed and an assessment made on their position in the market, and their financial strength. These should be linked to a summary of recent actions that illustrates the strategic direction that is being adopted by the company. Actions that increase market share by the introduction of new technology or business acquisition should be given full consideration and comments made upon how this will impact the business (Table 2.5).

Table 2.5 *Competitor profiles*

Competitor	Position (market/financial)	Actions recent/anticipated	Company response
Martin	Market leader with 26%	Forming an alliance with Abbey to dominate systems	Work to form European partnership
Haley	Dominate in Europe with 15% of the market	Focusing upon aerospace, moving away from trucks	Develop in-house new range of servo-valves
Lloyd	Currently hold 17% of market mainly in USA	Taken cash out of business to fund new venture	Consider acquisition to expand presence in USA

PRODUCT INTRODUCTION

The first requirement is to analyse the current product base to establish the life-cycle of the major product lines. If the majority of current products are in manufacture, with several requiring only aftermarket support, then the product introduction process will be critical for sustaining the business in future years.

Core Technologies

The business must identify the core technologies that are embodied within the current product base. These should be critically reviewed to establish how they can be commercially exploited in new products, with an assessment of in-house technology compared to major competitors. The key technology drivers should be determined to establish where to focus the development activities, together with economic and technical factors that are shaping the market. The technology requirements are often dictated by alternative product concepts emerging for the next generation of products. These must be fully understood and evaluated to determine those technologies that must be available for the company to compete and protect the existing customer base. A business can acquire new technology through a number of routes, but it is important to identify strategic core technologies that are critical to long-term viability. These must be fully developed and the intellectual property zealously protected from competition.

Technology Route Map

The mechanism for identifying a relevant technology programme is through the development of a route map. This technique uses the market demand to establish key elements of technology that have to be addressed. These can then be populated with a number of information blocks, the length of each block representing the time frame, with connecting arrows indicating the technology path. This technique provides a visual means of highlighting the key technical requirements, the level of technology interdependence, and the time frames available to ensure new products are released on time to meet the market demand. An example for the Aerospace market is shown in Figure 2.3.

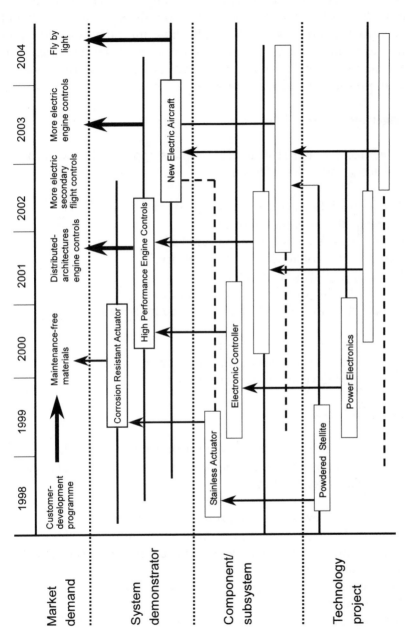

Figure 2.3 Technology route map

The development of new products in many industries is being undertaken in collaboration with other companies. Therefore, not all the new technology needs to be developed in-house, but it is essential to identify the *core technologies* the business must develop and retain if it is to secure a dominant business presence. These basic technologies may be referred to as *generic*, but are only one aspect of the overall product introduction process.

Product Introduction Plan

Another technique that structures business opportunities is a product introduction plan that identifies:

- The immediate customer and the customer chain;
- Name of the programme or product;
- Components/subsystems to be supplied;
- Partners and collaborators in the project;
- Dates of key project milestones;
- Potential value of sales to the company;
- Project status with level of customer commitment.

This approach is shown by the chart of Table 2.6, which displays the level of market opportunities, and the commitments made to major customers for developing new products.

Project Summaries

A brief description should be given for priority projects (class 1 or 2) and significant generic technology projects. This summary should provide details concerning:

- Reasons for developing the product or component;
- Benefits that will be derived from investing in the development;
- The advances in technology or changes in the market situation making it attractive;
- The customer requirements that will be satisfied;
- The financial opportunity;
- New features making the product commercially viable;
- Technical challenge that have to be addressed;
- Opportunities for exploiting the technology in other applications/ markets.

Table 2.6 *The product introduction plan*

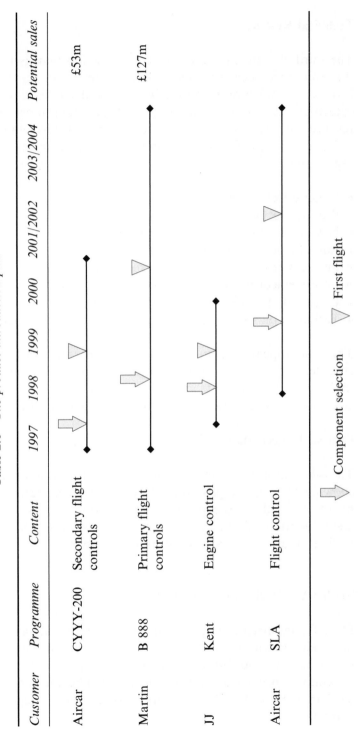

Customer	Programme	Content	1997	1998	1999	2000	2001/2002	2003/2004	Potential sales
Aircar	CYYY-200	Secondary flight controls							£53m
Martin	B 888	Primary flight controls							£127m
JJ	Kent	Engine control							
Aircar	SLA	Flight control							

⇨ Component selection   ▷ First flight

Technical Resources

The third element of the product introduction plan is to determine the level of technical resources needed to undertake the programmes. Product introduction resources have to be deployed in a number of categories, and cost estimates established that must include the resources needed for both product and process development.

The categories of work to be analysed from a resource requirement aspect are:

● Generic technology;
● Product development;
● New applications of existing products;
● Enhancements to existing products;
● Problem resolution and service support;
● Improvement projects to reduce manufacturing cost;
● Engineering services for testing and evaluation;
● Technical publications documentation and service documents.

This list appears exhaustive, but all the categories have to be considered and costed in order to obtain an accurate assessment of the overall product introduction resources required. A summary chart should be generated by category as shown in Table 2.7.

Current Project Status

The other information to be presented is a chart (Figure 2.4 on p. 38) showing the relative positions of development projects, against the phases defined by the product introduction process. This simply identifies the stage projects are at, demonstrating that the plan is realistic and making best use of finite resources.

SUPPLY-CHAIN MANAGEMENT

Plans for improving supply-chain operational performance can only be developed with an in-depth knowledge of the current manufacturing processes and future business strategy. The type of change programme needed to improve operational performance to a standard that meets the stakeholders' expectations is dependent upon many factors:

Table 2.7 *Technical resources proforma*

Classification	Programme	Status	1998		1999		2000		Customer/ funding source
			£m	%fund	£m	%fund	£m	%fund	
	Generic technology								
	Sub-total								
	Product development								
	Sub-total								
	New applications								
	Sub-total								
	Product enhancement								
	Sub-total								
	Problem resolution								
	Sub-total								
	Improvement projects								
	Sub-total								
	Engineering services								
	Sub-total								
	TOTAL committed								
	TOTAL investment								

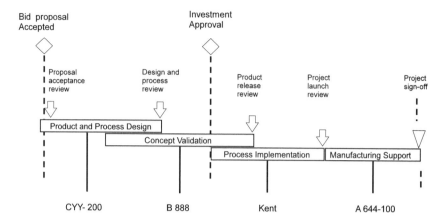

Figure 2.4   Project status

- Market sector being served;
- Geographical location of facilities;
- State of the manufacturing facilities and capacity available;
- Level of investment in capital equipment;
- Robustness of the product base;
- Skill of the workforce;
- Availability of training in core skills;
- Strength of the supply base.

However, the issues that must be addressed have a common foundation, and therefore it is important to understand:

- What is the customer purchasing from the company?
- Which components and elements of the manufacturing process are core to the business, and must be retained in-house to protect proprietary knowledge?
- What is the most cost-effective manufacturing system to meet the customer's requirements?

A statement should be made that summarises the background of the industrial sector and the factors that have influenced particular characteristics of the present supply-chain process. The main areas for improvement in performance should be identified together with changes in customer and business expectations that must be satisfied to remain a serious competitor.

Present Situation

A summary should be included that reviews the approach taken to restructuring the supply chain and changes that have been implemented. These may include items such as:

- Strategic make versus buy review to focus upon core components;
- Consolidation of manufacturing facilities;
- Restructuring operations focusing upon assembly and test within particular territories;
- Transfer of core machining to more appropriate locations;
- Opening new manufacturing facilities to secure expanding market opportunities;
- Restructuring the supply chain with investment in new manufacturing processes to protect core technologies.

Operational Improvement

Strategic ambition has to be tempered with the short-term supply chain operational improvements that are fundamental to profitability, and ensuring a cost structure that allows the business to survive. The first issue is available capacity, and possible duplication of resources across different sites. Over the past few years, simplified products, new manufacturing processes and international competition has possibly resulted in over capacity, and too many sites. One task therefore is to establish manufacturing locations and a matrix of core components to identify duplication of facilities (Table 2.8 and Figure 2.5). Sites must have sufficient workload to justify proposed capital investment, and duplicated manufacturing resources should be reviewed, taking action to consolidate excess capacity and to reduce fixed overheads. This should be linked to understanding which facilities manufacture the core components, and identifying any critical items that could seriously damage the business if the technology, or components, were only available from a major competitor.

Once a site-location strategy has been established, then various elements of the supply-chain process must to be designed to enhance operational performance. The internal supply chain must focus upon producing core components, assembly, test and aftermarket support. The manufacturing facilities must be modular, designed to satisfy the customer's requirements, maintaining a consistent flow of work through the cells and operating with minimum lead-time. The supply-chain product base should be analysed in terms of:

Table 2.8 *Sites – key information*

Location	Country	Activities on site	Area sq m.	People	Annual sales 1999 forecast	Main products
Flight Controls						
New York	USA	Business development Product introduction Supply chain	18 845	542	£45m	Secondary flight controls
Bristol	UK	Business development Supply chain Aftermarket	5 400	341	£24m	Primary flight controls
Valves						
Sheffield	UK	Business development Product introduction	12 680	600	£54m	Hydraulic valves
Derby	UK	Supply chain	6 000	440	£14m	Electric motors and controllers
Paris	France	Product introduction Supply chain	15 572	893	£39m	Solenoid valves

Core components	New York	Bristol	Sheffield	Derby	Paris
Test	■	■	■	■	■
Assembly	■	■	■	■	■
Body machining	■	■	■	▲	▲
Gears – straight	▲	■	■	▲	
Gears – bevel	■	■	▲		
Shafts	■	■			
Servo-valves	+	+	+	+	
Transducers	+	+	+	+	
Electric motors			▲	■	▲
Printed circuits	+	+	▲		■
Bearings	▲			■	+
Hydraulic pumps	▲		■		
Pistons	▲	■	▲		■
Valve blocks	■	■	▲		■
Seals/gaskets		▲	▲		■

■ Manufactured in-house ▲ Supplied from another factory
+ Purchased item

Figure 2.5 Core components used in the product portfolio

- *Runners* – items that are in regular production, of relatively high volumes, having all tooling and process planning information available.
- *Repeaters* – items that have a process plan, and are produced in batches at consistent intervals.
- *Strangers* – items having the minimum of process planning, usually 'geriatric' spares, prototypes or one-off project work.

Different manufacturing systems are needed, depending upon the type of components. It is important to engineer appropriate manufacturing modules/cells, that create a flow of work in a rhythm that paces the factory (Figure 2.6).

42

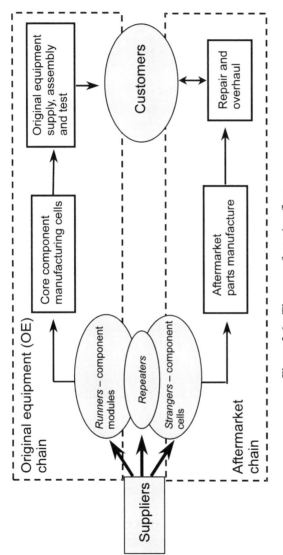

Figure 2.6 The manufacturing flow

Aspects of the supply-chain process to be assessed when developing a manufacturing policy are:

- *Make vs buy analysis* establishing the cost of bought out items and those manufactured in-house. The make vs buy decision must be regarded as strategic and not a short-term expedience to reduce product costs.
- *Structure the supply-chain* into runner, repeater and stranger products, with separate manufacturing systems for servicing different market/volume requirements. (Original equipment and possibly a broader service/aftermarket customer base.)
- *Cellular organisation structures,* identifying natural working groups to take full responsibility for all activities needed for completing a component or process.
- *Master production scheduling procedures* at three levels to establish the demand across the factory and with suppliers.
- *Demand-driven material flow systems,* pulling components through into assembly, shortening lead-times, reducing stock and work in progress, making problems visible and removing tolerance of failure.
- *Changeover times reduction,* introducing specialist equipment and procedures to support the changeover process.
- *Continuous improvement* through a relentless drive to eliminate all forms of waste.
- *Process capability of machine tools,* measuring equipment, materials processing, and assembly and test systems, through the application of statistical methods and experimental techniques to resolve problems.
- *Documentation for all processes and procedures,* making them user-friendly, supported by graphical/pictorial representation to aid understanding.
- *Materials handling,* introducing higher cleanliness levels and using dedicated containers to protect components as they move through the supply chain.
- *Modern IT systems* for manufacturing planning and control, giving real-time information on work-flow and manufacturing priorities.

Selecting the areas that provide the greatest overall business benefit is a critical management decision. Deficiencies in these areas can be identified using checklists to highlight gaps against known best practice. Ranking them and assessing the relative return requires considerable management judgment.

Purchasing

A professional supplies module is fundamental to achieving aggressive cost reductions, as more non-strategic items are purchased from quality assured, preferred suppliers. Most businesses spend over 65 per cent of revenue on purchased items. The product introduction process requires the greatest purchasing expertise, establishing a competitive supplier base for future products, but the continual drive for cost reductions to meet operational targets will only be achieved through consistently seeking ways of reducing the overall costs of raw materials, consumable items and services. A plan should be established to identify the categories of components with the greatest spend profiles, or most significant supplier problems, and ranked in priority order for improving business performance. The total company spend on selected commodity groups should be assigned to one person with responsibility for achieving improved supplier performance linked to significant total acquisition-cost reductions.

Table 2.9 *Analysis of spending*

Commodity	Spend £m	Number of suppliers	Number of suppliers – 80% of spend	Target cost savings %	Performance rating – cost quality delivery
Castings	£4.6m	20	8	10%	70%
Bearings	£2.8m	8	4	4%	90%
Machining	£15.8m	35	19	12%	60%

DISTRIBUTION AND AFTERMARKET

The distribution of products as they leave the manufacturing centre, has become a significant factor in creating competitor advantage. New ways of reaching the end customer are being exploited with changing customer purchasing habits. Therefore, the first aspect to consider is the route products take to market. This can be illustrated by charting the various ways a product reaches the end customers, and establishing the split in product volumes going through various channels (Figure 2.7). The next requirement is to understand the

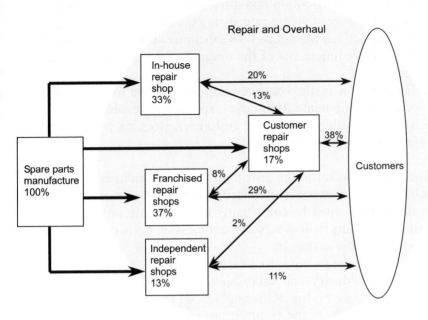

Figure 2.7   The flow of spare parts to airline customers

leadtime taken for the products to reach the end customer and develop an appropriate logistics strategy that ensures the pipeline contains the minimum level of stock, whilst guaranteeing the service levels expected by the market. The logistic systems required for new product and aftermarket parts may be different, therefore it is important to understand the dynamics and customers' requirements of both market segments.

The relative importance of the original equipment and aftermarket elements of the business is dependent upon the type of products, position in the value chain, and the proportion of sales and profit generated through the aftermarket business. However, it is important to understand the profitability of service parts, because while the reselling prices may be considerably higher, the reported manufacturing and distribution costs may not capture all the invisible cost of disruption within the supply-chain process.

In some industries, the distribution and aftermarket support is organised as a separate business. Consequently, this section of the business plan is a microcosm of the overall plan and has to address:

- The role of distribution and aftermarket in the overall business;
- Market changes that are influencing the different market segments;
- Specific actions being taken by customers within the value chain;
- Differing requirements of the original equipment and service-part customers;
- The position of the company and the relative market shares for original equipment, aftermarket, spares and repairs;
- The relationship with major customers, stocking policies and key factors that influence sales.

The primary factor in the distribution and aftermarket process is the achievement of industry standard customer service levels. Delivery promise dates must be consistently met to secure ongoing business, and a company will not survive unless it performs at the level expected by the customer.

Therefore, the plan has to identify benchmark performance targets within the industry and establish the actions and implementation projects necessary for achieving an upper quartile performance. Exhibits to support the commentary could include a list of performance measures that establish target delivery performance levels and order replenishment lead-times to be achieved by key dates within the plan.

BUSINESS SUPPORT

A process-driven organisation may be structured at various levels:

- *Manufacturing unit* managed by an operations manager;
- *Business unit* that supports a range of products and customers managed by a general manager;
- *Head office* integrating a number of businesses controlled by the managing director.

Elements of the business process may be distributed across different locations. However, the key to ensuring the effective running of the overall business is the support provided by three staff activities that operate in a matrix mode across the business processes. These people have the important role of integrating the overall process, taking responsibility to ensure critical aspects of the business are given full management support, key business performance para-meters are measured and controlled, and the commitments made in the plan are delivered. The three staff roles needed to support the business processes are:

- Customer satisfaction and quality;
- Project management;
- Financial management and control.

These three roles will be described in the following sections. Staff appointments are not required at every location or in each local management team, but an appropriate structure is needed to ensure that integrated management activities are fully understood and action will be taken to address and implement decisions.

CUSTOMER SATISFACTION AND QUALITY

This person represents the customer within the management team and has responsibility for ensuring that all quality standards and legal requirements are consistently met. The role is to establish the quality process and procedures within the organisation, defining the route map for confirming that all components and products fully comply with the specification. It also provides the customer focus essential for identifying and improving those elements of performance the customer regards as important.

Initiatives that have been adopted by some businesses include:

- 'Putting your customer first' programmes;
- Establishing product-integrity review boards to assess product performance;
- Introducing quality route maps to establish the gaps in overall quality performance and initiating plans for improvement;
- Investigating root causes of product failures and introducing corrective actions;
- Organising change projects for improving critical aspects of quality performance.

The essential tool for underpinning this activity is a series of performance measures that monitors the customers' views and the costs of poor quality. These should include the following.

The Customers' View

- Customer reports on actual performance compared to other major competitors, for quality, delivery and cost.
- A monitor of customer perception that gives qualitative measures of the customers' attitudes/acceptance of the company.

Costs Associated with Quality

- Cost of internal quality-assurance activities.
- Cost of all internal scrap and rework.
- Cost of external failure, including the service element required to support the product in the field.

These costs may be expressed as a ratio against manufacturing costs, sales or profit, to provide a non-dimensional figure used for monitoring trends.

Product Service Information

- Number of units returned from customers.
- Meantime between failure for units in service.
- Concessions raised in the supply chain allowing non-conforming components to be used in production.
- Number of design changes introduced to current products over a specified period.
- Incidents or occurrences in the field associated with a malfunction of the company's product.

Delivery Performance

- The service level achievement, monitoring the required deliveries against the actual shipments.
- The lead time for shipping goods to the customer from the receipt of an order.
- Supplier performance:

  ○ quality,
  ○ delivery, and
  ○ cost.

The range of measures used across different industries and types of business will vary, but the important feature is to agree a common set of measures, with definitions for quantifying the information on a routine basis. This discipline provides visibility for the customers' requirements and the occurrence of non-scheduled events that may have a detrimental impact upon the customer.

PROGRAMME MANAGEMENT

The majority of resources in a business are committed to operational activities. This normally involves using a number of complex procedures that have evolved over several years, and which are the foundation of the business process. The role of the programme manager is to ensure adequate time and investment is given to the design and implementation of new processes and products needed to maintain a competitive position in the market. Project management is the primary mechanism for driving change through a business and is fundamental to defining the magnitude of the task, determining key milestones, and the costs associated with implementing change.

Projects are generally undertaken by a multi-disciplinary team of people with the skills necessary to design new products and processes and to take responsibility for implementing the changes. Therefore, the business planning process is the mechanism whereby a management team agree critical objectives that must be achieved to secure the future viability of the business. It is the responsibility of the programme manager to ensure the *cost* of these projects is accurately determined, can be afforded by the business and provides adequate returns on the total investment. Projects are usually assigned to teams that take responsibility for designing and implementing changes within scheduled time scales.

Projects should encompass all the business processes and should be aimed at providing a step change in performance, backed by a continuous improvement activity for sustaining the changes. The product introduction process should also be part of the programme management responsibility to ensure projects are costed, adequately resourced and progressing to plan. The role of the programme manager is to provide direct management involvement in the project teams, and ensure any hazards to the budget or delivery schedule are given full management attention.

Within this section, the programme manager should provide outline information concerning:

- The project management process;
- The rules and outline parameters for raising hazards reports;
- A list of top priority projects that will be reported to the programme office giving information on:
  - the project owners responsible for implementation,
  - objectives and deliverables for the key projects,
  - a cost and benefits statement ensuring projects provide adequate return, and
  - a summary of resources required and the availability of people.

In the business plan, details of the projects should be listed on a summary chart. However, all projects must be underpinned with a standard set of documentation that provide a project summary, a project plan with the time scales for achieving key milestones, plus a resource and expenditure statement. A typical list is shown in Table 2.10 for an Aerospace business.

The key to successful projects is to assign full-time project managers, and introduce a monthly reporting procedure that provides information on the progress made towards delivering the key milestones within the authorised budgeted costs. These monthly reports need to be supported by a *hazard* reporting mechanism that provides an escalation route for any problem that could adversely impact the project, causing it to slip beyond agreed limits.

FINANCIAL MANAGEMENT AND CONTROL

The finance activity has responsibility for imposing strict financial controls and management reporting disciplines. Reporting procedures must be robust, providing management with accurate information necessary to take executive decisions. The reporting systems employed at the various levels should provide sufficient detail for local management, and for hands-on senior management, facilitating consolidation at higher levels.

Financial management must ensure:

- forecasting routines are capable of predicting financial performance with a high degree of confidence;

Table 2.10 Project summaries

Project description	Project owner	Objectives and deliverables	Start date	Finish date	Cost of project	Benefits
Business development						
US valve market	P. Allen	Obtain 20% share of the US market worth £29m	Jan. '98	Dec. '98	£1.5m	Expand the available market
Martin alliance	K. Law	Gain access to B 888 flight control programme	Mar. '98	Nov. '98	£0.4m	Increase market share to leader position
Aircar SLA	T. Rush	Win next generation flight control using new materials	Sep. '98	April '99	£1.2m	Retain position as no. 1 supplier
Product introduction						
Aircar CYYY-200 flight control	J. Brown	Provide fully qualified flight control system	April '98	Sept. '02	£3.4m	Consolidate market lead
J.J. Kent upgrade	C. Rank	Extend the life of engine	Aug. '98	Dec. '00	£2.7m	Keep business
Supply chain						
Relocate Sheffield	I. Wilts	Establish one machining operation in Bristol	Feb. '98	Feb. '99	£4.1m	Remove excess capacity
Redesign Bristol	J. Shaw	Introduce manufacturing modules and remove cost	Sept. '98	Sept. '99	£0.6m	Make valve business viable
Aftermarket/distribution						
Establish world distribution centre	F. Khan	Combine existing four units into single unit	Jan. '98	Nov. '99	£1.8m	Reduce overheads

- financial reports are available immediately at the end of the accounting period, with time allocated to analysing results and making recommendations;
- control mechanisms are effective to restrict the outflow of cash and maintain working capital within planned levels;
- reported figures are accurate, avoiding any possibility of double-counting profits;
- auditing procedures are routine with any figures presented in the accounts accurately reflecting the business position; and
- costing systems that allow accurate comparisons.

The financial manager must have a plan for implementing the changes needed to improve the accounting disciplines, but within the context of the business plan; he or she takes responsibility for collating and providing the financial information needed to support the business case.

The type of exhibits that should be presented, giving information on the past two years' performance, actual and budgeted costs for the current year, and projections over the plan period with benchmark targets and dates, are as follows:

Financial Summary

- Sales;
- Trading profit;
- Restructuring and costs of major project charges;
- Redundancy and closure costs.

  $\implies$ *Profit before interest and tax*
  $\implies$ *Operating cash flow*

- Closing cash balance;
- Employees – year-end, average in year; and
- Payroll costs.

Key Ratios

- Return on sales;
- Capital turnover ratio;
- Return on capital employed;
- Sales/employee;
- Added value per £ payroll cost;

- Payroll costs % sales;
- Capital expenditure;
- Depreciation;
- Engineering costs;
- Engineering funding.

⟹ *Net engineering costs*

- Third-party trade debtors at year's end;
- Gross stocks – year's end;
- Gross stock to sales ratio;
- Break-even sales/sales %.

Performance against Previous Plan on Critical Factors

- Sales and profit variance analysis year over year;
- Cash flow and closing cash balances;
- Key ratios: ROS, ROCE, CTR, sales per employee, added value per £ of pay, payroll costs % sales, stock to sales.

Sales and Profit Variance analysis – Year over Year and to Last Financial Plan

Impact upon Sales

- Change in revenue streams by product family: original equipment and spares, analysing the impact of volume, mix of products and pricing;
- Associated companies, including acquisitions and divestment;
- Impact of exchange rates.

⟹ *Total change*

Impact upon Profit before Interest and Tax

- Cost recovery: volume, mix, pricing and impact of exchange rates;
- Changes in material and bought out prices;
- Changes in payroll costs: wage inflation, numbers employed, total wage bill;
- Change non-payroll overheads costs: facilities and equipment, selling and distribution overheads;
- Product introduction costs: generic technology, new product development, supporting existing products;

- Other factors: exchange rates, restructuring, royalties, provisions, contingencies, acquisitions, divestments and so forth.

  $\Longrightarrow$ *Total change*

Cash Flow Statement

- Provides statements for profit before interest and tax, share of associated companies depreciation, capital investment, changes in working capital (movement of stocks, debtors, creditors) and effect of major investments.

  $\Longrightarrow$ *Operating cash flow*

- Interest paid/received, leasing interest, dividends, investment and divestment – to establish the cash generated/used – plus a statement on the borrowings movement.

  $\Longrightarrow$ *Opening and closing cash balances*

Other information will include:

- **Risks and opportunities** for increasing/decreasing sales and profit.
- **Profit and loss account**.
- **Balance sheet**.
- **Employee/payroll costs**.
- **Product introduction costs by programme**.
- **Capital expenditure** for new products, manufacturing capacity, quality, safety/environmental, productivity, cost-reduction, replacement equipment, plus other items including tooling, information technology, cars, land and buildings and so on.
- **Stock analysis and stock to sales ratios**; in particular the value of stock – analysis by raw materials, work in progress, maintenance, consumable materials, finished goods, and replacement parts.
- **Third-party trade debtors** with an analysis by value, and days of outstanding customer payments.

The financial data presented will vary from business to business, depending upon the drivers and the performance measures favoured by the senior executive team. However, the purpose of the financial information is to provide details of how the business is currently performing, establishing future financial commitments that will be made to the company directors.

Financial Performance

The financial performance should be reviewed, summarising the budget that the management team are committed to delivering and presenting for board approval. The information must highlight the key business performance projections over the plan period and give an explanation as to how the financial commitments will be achieved. An analysis is also required examining major variances from the previous plans, with reasons and detailed explanations for any changes.

BUSINESS STRATEGY AND ACTIONS

The final section of the business plan should focus upon the business strategy and other policies that are required to secure the future viability of the business. This should be owned and compiled by the general manager, addressing:

Strategy Development

- *The position of the business in the industry*, comparing the size of the business with other companies, its ability to compete effectively and the relationship with competitors.
- *Activities across the industry* that are impacting available capacity, reasons for expansion or consolidation, the cost pressures within the industry, potential acquisitions, divestments or alliances, and actions being taken by competitors to secure commercial advantage.
- *Strengths, weaknesses, opportunities and threats* analysis for the business, demonstrating the potential for growth and actions that must be taken to retain stakeholder value.
- *Commentary by major or potential market territory* on the investments made, and actions the company will take in relation to the political and economic factors in particular areas of the world. Consideration should also be given to the structure of industry, location of manufacturing sites, status of local manufacturers and the reputation of the business.
- *List of potential acquisitions divestments*, and alliances giving the name of the parent company, company name, sales revenue and making the business case.

- *Vision of the business* and its position within the industry, describing the critical actions that are necessary to accurately position the business.
- *Role* of the business within the company portfolio;
- *Strategy and goals* that have been established for the business.
- *Policies* that must be implemented to sustain a viable business, and satisfy its role.
- *Critical success factors* that must be achieved to meet the business challenges.
- *Business performance objectives* that must be delivered, including financial commitments and significant projects.
- *Tactical actions* necessary to be a successful management team.

Organisation Structure

The critical task for the general manager is to change the organisation from a traditional functional structure into a process-based organisation that works as a team. This requires the key business process management roles to be defined, together with the supporting structure needed to integrate the processes (Figure 2.8).

Figure 2.8 A process-based organisation

The general manager must identify and assign someone with responsibility for each business process. A person may manage more that one process, depending upon the size of the task and the organisation in other parts of the company structure designed to support specific business processes.

Organisation Principles

A statement should be prepared that outlines how the organisation will approach:

- Employee development;
- Payment and reward systems;
- Resource levels;
- Methods of working; and
- Training and skills requirements

This information can be presented in charts and tables that audits the present situation.

Management Development

This defines how people's performance will be assessed and individual development plans established to improve effectiveness. It also examines the management team's overall ability to deliver the business plan and identifies a mechanism for succession planning. A statement should also be made on how young people with potential are being developed with any deficiencies in the skill base identified and corrected.

Information Technology

Its use is critical to the effectiveness of the organisation and is an essential tool for supporting change within the organisation. Therefore, it is important to establish the hardware and software standards that will be adopted across the companies to facilitate the ready access of information. Consideration must be given to:

- Programme management and reporting system;
- Marketing and customer database;
- Product data management;

- Configuration management and change control;
- Computer aided design;
- Product and process analysis tools;
- Production planning and control systems;
- Commercial systems;
- Financial planning and reporting systems;
- Personnel systems;
- Customer satisfaction and quality systems;
- Customer service systems for product literature, manuals and documentation;
- Word processing, spreadsheet and presentation packages;
- Networks and communication.

Summary of Objectives and Actions

This section summarises the strategy and business objectives identified in the plan, and states the actions and people responsible for delivering quantified business benefits.

Non-financial Business Measures of Performance

Here are listed the key non-financial performance measures that will be used to monitor and control the business, providing details of current performance, the plan, budget commitments and benchmark targets that will be achieved within the time span of the plan.

Note: A recommended layout for a business plan is to start each section on a new page, inserting a sheet of illustrations and tables, facing the appropriate page of text.

3

Customer Development Process

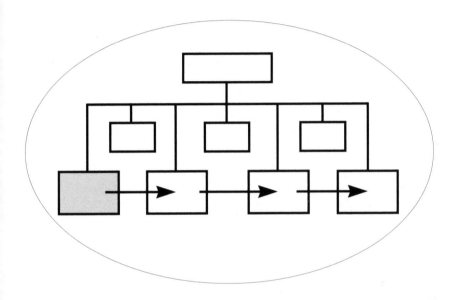

Topics

Introduction
Market overview
Market forecast
Business intelligence system
Opportunity evaluation
Identify the opportunity
Evaluation of requirements
Product and project approval
Bid preparation
Winning the contract
Summary

3

Customer Development Process

INTRODUCTION

The process for identifying customer needs and winning orders is probably the least well-defined business process. It also has the widest spectrum of techniques for accomplishing the task. The process described in this section is based upon a high-technology manufacturing company seeking to move up the supply chain, providing products and services with a higher value-added content. It aims to outline an effective set of procedures ensuring the finite resources available to secure new business are targeted at the best opportunities in the marketplace to meet the strategic objectives of the business.

MARKET OVERVIEW

The market overview for a particular industry sector, prepared for the business plan, provides the foundation for customer development. The overall market available to the company is examined in relation to the segments that are important to the business. Detailed information is then collated, relative to the range of products within the portfolio, to identify:

- The major market segments that have a significant impact upon the business.
- The prime factors that drive the market and the key buying factors.
- World and national trends that will have an influence upon the market (for example growth in GDP, ageing population in industrialised countries).
- Movement in specific market segments due to new technologies, changes in the demand patterns, trends in fashion, changes in strategies and methods of operating.
- Major events that influence national and international perception and requirements.

- New legislation that specifies cleaner, safer, more environmentally-friendly products and manufacturing processes.
- Customer demands creating pressures for increased functionality, quality and reliability without a significant increase in price.
- Social trends.
- Impact of new technologies that provide alternative more cost effective solutions.
- Influence of competitors seeking to re-position themselves in the value chain.
- Movements in monetary policy and exchange rates.
- Related economic factors that influence the market (for example new building starts, increased wage rates, increased car sales).
- Privatisation of businesses injecting cash into the economy.
- Takeovers, mergers and industrial consolidation.
- Global sourcing that is changing the value chain and redistributing wealth creation.

This information should be tabulated and analysed to determine which events will have the greatest impact upon the business's markets. Exhibits can then be prepared showing an overview of the market with quantified data over a relevant time span, say the past three years, the current year's forecast, and projections for the next five years. This high level information can be calibrated from a number of sources for particular industries, but ultimately it is the responsibility of the person who owns the business development process to provide definitive figures that will be used by the business.

MARKET FORECAST

The market overview has to be transformed into a business market forecast, which requires the information to be translated into financial statements defining the key market segments and the business's sales potential. Each factor that may impact the market segment must be reviewed, and a judgment taken, in order to provide a fully calibrated market forecast. In some instances the major original equipment manufacturers provide component suppliers with a forecast of requirements for the ongoing business, but these need to be verified against the business's own market overview to factor out over-optimistic projections. This market analysis identifies the relative size and growth within each market segment, but the most important task is to establish a process for identifying prospective business on new programmes. Gathering the necessary intelligence needed to identify customers' future requirements is an essential part of the overall marketing process, and is based upon having an intimate knowledge of particular industry sectors. However, the most reliable source of information is through direct customer contacts, and developing well-established relationships that encourage partici-pation at the conceptual stage of new products. The task of the marketing group is to generate an informed list of prospective opportunities to be considered when preparing the company's busi-ness plan and determining strategies (Table 3.1).

BUSINESS INTELLIGENCE SYSTEM

General information on businesses is readily available from a number of sources (newspaper reports, the Internet, company news sheets, analysts' reports, companies' annual reports), but this needs to be refined to provide specific information on particular businesses, or groups of activities. Collecting and analysing business information must be structured and routinely updated. The most reliable and useful source of information is from meetings held with companies; visit reports should be mandatory, following contact with end-users, customers, competitors and partners.

The type of information that needs to be collected and made available will cover the following areas:

- Company; division; location.
- Main product lines; core activities on site.
- Person contacted; job title; area of prime responsibility.
- Name and position of key decision-makers on site.
- Number of people employed on site.
- Sales turnover by product line.
- Main customers' products and services provided.
- Value of sales by product line for the business.
- Customer perception, relationships between companies, quality status, cost performance, and delivery achievement.
- State of the customer's business.
- Opportunities to develop and grow existing business.
- New developments that could provide additional business.
- Key time scales for introducing new technology and products.

Table 3.1 Prospective development projects proforma

Customer	Programme	Items to be supplied	Bid date	Prototype date	Launch date	Sales value £m	Major competitors	Project attractiveness	Chance of winning

It is the responsibility of everybody in the organisation to contribute towards building comprehensive databases on customers, competitors, partners, and any relevant emerging technologies. This information can be summarised for a number of purposes: management contacts, company profiles, vendor ratings, feedback to product line managers, developing future product strategies and formulating business plans. The IT systems for structuring this data are not as well-developed as those used to support other business processes, but are crucial for growing the business and establishing the necessary links with customers. PC-based data management packages can be used effectively to simplify processing of information, making it readily accessible to people across the organisation.

One approach companies are taking for promoting the collection and dissemination of information on businesses is to formalise the circulation of regular internal company reports concerning key customers and competitors. These reports can also be used to provide a vendor rating system, communicating good performance and highlighting under-achievement.

OPPORTUNITY EVALUATION

The organisation of customer development activities must be dependent upon the business needs, but with markets becoming global a balance must be achieved between planning to exploit an opportunity centrally using a common solution, or working locally and adding variety allowing territorial requirements to be accommodated. The practice of using customer account managers working within a team environment is becoming an accepted way for developing relationships at all levels within an organisation, strengthening the position for winning new business across the range of possible applications and understanding the overall customers' requirements. However, the commitment to introduce a new product can be a significant business undertaking that puts the future viability of the company at risk, therefore an opportunity evaluation process for product introduction has to be defined. This consists of a number of phases as shown in Figure 3.1.

These events must complement the *Product Introduction Process*, providing an essential front end *Opportunity Evaluation* process, resulting in a commitment from the company to invest the resources needed to introduce a new product, and the commitment from a customer to place orders for the product.

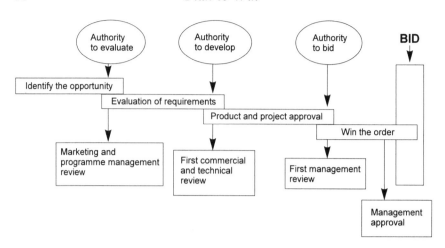

Figure 3.1 Opportunity evaluation

IDENTIFY THE OPPORTUNITY

The task of identifying opportunities is a combination of establishing customer strategies and targeting specific projects on which to seek new business, but in all instances it requires:

- A full appreciation of the market requirements;
- Availability of technologies that meet the customer aspirations;
- An in-depth understanding of the customer;
- An evaluation of their position in the market;
- Identification of the supply chain and the ultimate customer requirement.

In component manufacturing industries, developing a close working relationship with the original equipment supplier, based upon a robust account plan, is the most successful way to secure both new and on-going business. The aim is to form partnerships with the customer by providing the technical specification and performance criteria needed to meet their needs. In some instances it is also possible to become a member of the customer's evaluation team, particularly when sharing the technical and commercial risk. Early visibility of potential opportunities is essential, and these need to be identified ahead of the business planning cycle in order to develop business strategies and establish priorities for the allocation of finite commercial and technical resources (see Figure 3.2).

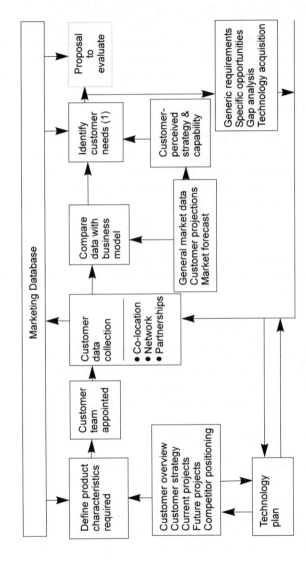

Figure 3.2 Opportunity evaluation phase 1: identify the opportunity ⟶ proposal to evaluate

The marketing group is responsible for identifying the range of opportunities that are available to the business, but this list has to be refined and a judgment made on the projects that should be selected for further evaluation. In many instances the projects are self-selecting resulting from existing relationships that exist between the two companies. However, in order to support a recommendation to evaluate particular projects, marketing and programme management should make an initial commercial assessment based upon the best current information. Aspects that should be reviewed include:

- *Demand expectations*:

    o short and long term sales volumes;
    o revenues using various product cost structures, based upon volume and different manufacturing routes;
    o time to respond to customers' needs;
    o demand patterns due to seasonal requirements and fashion;
    o rate of likely repeat orders;
    o length of product life-cycle;
    o speed of customer acceptance;
    o growth rate for the new product in replacing existing components.

- *Cost expectations*:

    o product unit costs that must be achieved;
    o use of existing resources and technology;
    o level of non-recurring expenditure required for development;
    o economics of scale and experience.

- *Competitive conditions*:

    o short and long-term market share;
    o lead-time over other competitors and the time needed to imitate the product;
    o the strengths and weaknesses of the business;
    o possible new entrants into the market;
    o reactions of competitors and likely actions.

- *Pricing*:

    o value-based pricing, economic value to the customer, and whole life costs;

o pricing policies to support the product strategy;
o discounts structure to achieve potential sales targets;
o promotional pricing and product launch costs.

- *Investment requirements*:

  o product introduction expenses including test rigs;
  o additional production plant and equipment;
  o production facilities;
  o promotional events and advertising;
  o distribution facilities, logistics and storage.

- *Profitability*:

  o cash flow and the recovery of development costs;
  o short and long-term business profitability;
  o internal return on investment;
  o level of commercial and technical risk.

The information from this first phase study should be formally collated and presented at an appropriate marketing and programme management review that has the authority to make the decision to *evaluate the opportunity* and assign the funds needed to progress to the next stage.

Collating this information takes significant effort, but extreme commercial rigour must be applied at this decision-point because the next phase consumes considerable valuable management resources. It is essential these are directed towards those projects providing the greatest opportunity for the business to deliver both its long and short-term strategies.

EVALUATION OF REQUIREMENTS

This phase of the process requires the participation of key people involved in the product introduction and supply chain processes, in addition to the members of the marketing and customer account management teams. Collectively they are responsible for managing the overall commitment required for new product introduction, balancing the position of the business in the market with the need to generate profits. A core team needs to be appointed that represents all aspects of the business to:

- Develop the draft product specification;
- Prepare the outline concept designs;
- Identify viable manufacturing methods;
- Prepare an outline project plan;
- Establish the initial project classification;
- Determine the technical and commercial risk;
- Identify and quantify the benefits available to the customer.
- Estimate the product and process development costs;
- Confirm the target product costs, based upon the initial concept designs;
- Identify possible cost reductions;
- Construct the projected sales and profit plan for the product; and
- Demonstrate the viability of any proposed new technology.

The process of evaluating requirements is summarised in Figure 3.3. Compiling this information and the report needed for the proposal to develop an opportunity takes considerable effort to assemble, and culminates with the first *commercial and technical review* for the project. It is recommended that a formal procedure is established with appropriate senior managers intimately involved in making the decision to proceed or not. This group must have the authority and available budget to make a commitment allowing the project to proceed to the next phase.

The approval to develop an opportunity formally registers the project, quantifying the critical aspects and associated costs. The information presented for review should be owned and managed by the marketing and commercial group, with appropriate involvement of the other areas, and must include:

- Quantified marketing and commercial information;
- Customer and competitor analysis;
- Confirmation that the opportunity meets the business-plan objectives, and supports the business's product and customer strategies;
- Outline product specification that is agreed and meets the customer's needs;
- Concept product designs that satisfy the specification and customer's requirements;
- Preliminary viable manufacturing methods and process routes for core components;
- Possible technical partners and key component suppliers;

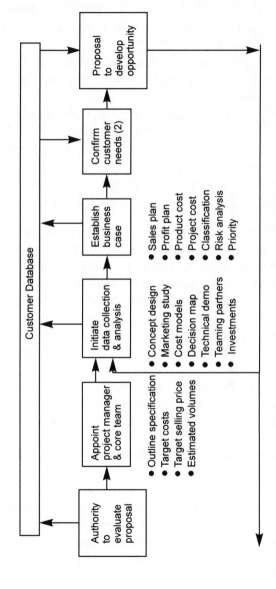

Figure 3.3 Phase 2: evaluation of requirements ⟶ proposal to develop opportunity

- Recommendations on quality systems and mandated legal requirements;
- Considered assessment of potential commercial risks and returns;
- Evaluation of the project's commercial parameters:
  o outline sales plan – new business, substitution of existing products,
  o profit potential – higher volumes, more efficient manufacture,
  o estimated product costs at product launch, and after gaining experience,
  o investment requirement in non-recurring expenditure, capital equipment, and working capital,
  o recoveries on expenditure – grants, partnerships, customer funds, and
  o cash flow and internal rate of returns;
- Summary of the overall project's risks and opportunities.

Following the review, the project should be formally signed off and an appropriate response made to the customer, detailing the business's decision. All proposals must be systematically summarised for the business management team to ensure they understand and support the project. In addition, the business management team must set overall priorities on where to focus resources relative to the other commitments, making sure finite technical and management resources are directed towards delivering the overall business objectives.

Once the project is approved, then a project manager must be assigned the task of championing and planning the project approval phase in preparation for making a bid proposal.

Project Classification – Risk Assessment

To support project selection and risk assessment for a variety of different opportunities, a *project classification* process is needed for comparing projects and establishing their relative level of commercial risk posed to the business. This can be achieved by scoring a number of critical factors, and using different weighting to give a quantified risk evaluation for the overall project. The purpose of developing a system is to provide a management tool based upon a series of control parameters that can be used to assess the level of risk and relative importance of different projects. This allows senior management to focus attention onto those projects having the highest scores,

Total Proposal Value
0–3m (Dev + OE +Spares) — 3 points
3–5 m — 10 points
Every 0.5m above 5m add — ADD 2 points

Estimated % ROS
>15% — 6 points
>10% <15% — 15 points
Every 2% below 10% add — ADD 3 points

Non-recurring costs
<1m — 4 points
>1m <2m — 9 points
Every 0.5m above add — ADD 4 points

Cash Flow
Break-even months
<24 months — 9 points
>24 <36 — 20 points
Every extra 6 months add — ADD 3 points

Max Cash Outlay
<1m — 5 points
>1m <3m — 12 points
Every 0.5m above £m — ADD 1 point

	Max Score	Project Score	Class Points	Classification Guidance 4	3	2	1
Total Proposal Value	25			4	6	12	16+
Estimated % ROS	20			6	8	10	12+
Non-recurring costs	14			5	6	8	10+
Cash Flow	30			6	10	16	20+
Max Cash Outlay	24			4	6	13	16+

Figure 3.4 Typical project classification chart

which implies having the greatest potential impact upon a business's profitability or a significant element of commercial risk. The scoring systems and relative weightings have to be tailored to specific businesses, but the example shown in Figure 3.4 shows the type of factors with typical values that should be used for assessing a project's classification.

This type of financial assessment has to be supported by a number of other factors that will influence the overall rating for the project. These are listed below, but need to be scored according to the impact and risks the management team consider they pose to the business.

(Points Guide – add points)

- *Specification:*
  - Is the specification subject to customer change?   8 points
  - Is the specification imprecise, vague or ambiguous?   8 points
  - Is it incomplete or awaiting additional information?   8 points

- *Product and process technology:*
  - Readily available without modifications   0 points
  - Design requires more than 30% modification to critical parameters   9 points
  - Design needs new concepts to realise potential   18 points
  - Relies on new technology   30 points
  - Beyond the current state of the technology   60 points

- *Customer:*
  - A new customer   10 points
  - Customer of strategic importance to the business   12 points
  - Location that will hinder communication   4 points
  - Difficult trading conditions   5 points
  - Customer milestones are unknown   10 points
  - Customer is a government department   12 points

- *Project schedule:*
  - Project unlikely to slip or miss key milestones   0 points
  - No risk of missing key customer dates   0 points
  - Risk factors likely to result in missing milestones but no risk to the customer   6 points
  - Risk factors likely to impact the customer schedule and programme at risk of missing customer launch dates   20 points

- *Customer schedule:*
  - o Customer programme influenced by external
    factors that could impact the programme   6 points
- *Skills requirement:*
  - o Low (required skills readily available)   0 points
  - o Average   8 points
  - o High (new skills required, dependent upon
    scarce skills)   18 points

The relative importance of these factors can only be determined by
the management team, and requires subjective judgment based upon
the critical factors that directly impact the business. Each factor
needs to be considered on its relative importance, and given a score
that reflects the impact it could have upon the business in terms of
potential risk. The total score then has to be calibrated using previous
projects to confirm that the scoring system identifies the relative
magnitude of risk, and if necessary values should be adjusted
accordingly. The scoring system should then be refined upon subsequent iterations and experience of using the system, until it proves a
reliable management tool. The aim should be to establish a range of
numerical scores for, say, *four categories* of project reflecting the
relative level of importance and risk the project pose to the business.
The first iteration of the project classification can be based upon
estimated values that are made more accurate as the project progresses. However, a project classification stays with the project
throughout the product introduction process, and is instrumental in
determining the levels of authority needed to allow the project to
proceed. Projects with the highest score are classified as *Class 1* and
need the highest level of authorisation with maximum senior management visibility and control due to the commercial risks they pose to
the business.

PRODUCT AND PROJECT APPROVAL

Once the decision has been taken to proceed with preparing a bid
proposal, then the objective is to win the business for the company.
Therefore, the task is to position everyone in the decision-making
chain into giving a positive vote for the project.

Winning the order is essentially a civilised battle, won by gathering intelligence, deploying a strategy and commitment beyond the call of duty.

This requires understanding customer requirements and creating strategies that take full account of the competitors' approaches to securing the business. This can be achieved through developing simulated competitor proposals, and creating 'red' and 'blue' team reviews that evaluate alternative scenarios. In practice, these techniques are found to be remarkably accurate and informative for developing winning proposals. The other important factor is to identify the customer 'champions' that will support the proposal and provide essential information on the critical features being sought by the customer. All these efforts must be coordinated and focused on the single objective of winning the business, but a close involvement with the customer in preparing the technical specification and setting the framework for the bid proposals is normally advantageous for the business. Companies must also strive to exploit all the influences and resources that are available, because contracts are awarded based upon a wide variety of factors.

Therefore, the task of preparing the information for the product and project approval takes considerable valuable business resources and must be the assigned responsibility of a project manager. If there is insufficient time, or if resources are not available, then the management team must decide the priorities on where to direct effort. Winning an inadequately defined programme may be far more damaging to the business than losing the job. This is the most critical stage of the customer development process, with activities focused upon developing the business plan for the product and obtaining the necessary authorisations needed to commit the company into making the financial investments required for delivering the programme (see Figure 3.5).

The first task for the project manager is creating a budget for the work packages required to prepare the product business plan and win the order. These funds must be identified within the company's business plan and the level of resources allocated to developing bid proposals agreed by the management team. Unless tightly controlled, there is always a tendency to chase too many opportunities, taking valuable resources away from delivering the projects critical to the business and compromising commitments already made to customers.

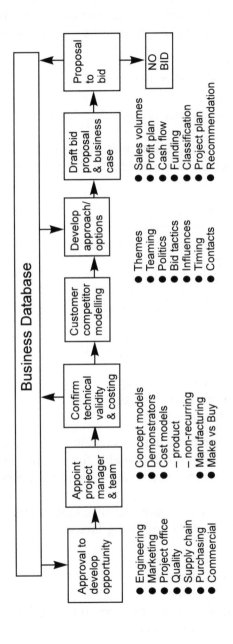

Figure 3.5 Phase 3: product and project approval ⟶ proposal to bid

A project manager takes overall responsibility for the project, preparing the technical and commercial information required for assessing the project viability and structuring the bid. The work packages needed to complete these tasks include the following:

Project Planning and Preparation

- Preparing a detailed cost estimate for delivering this phase of the project;
- Assembling a project team with full and part-time members, comprising people with knowledge and experience of the following disciplines:

  - product engineering,
  - manufacturing engineering,
  - purchasing and supplier development,
  - quality assurance,
  - marketing and product strategy,
  - commercial negotiations and contracts,
  - legal and contractual agreements,
  - customer-account management,
  - programme management and planning,
  - cost-estimating,
  - finance and business planning,
  - production control and logistics, and
  - supply-chain management;

- Developing a time-phased project plan with the key milestones based upon the time-frame available for submitting the bid;
- Obtaining management approval to spend the necessary funds.

This team then prepares a comprehensive business plan, providing an objective assessment of the following factors:

Technical and Cost Evaluation

- The *technical specification* and operating envelope, as confirmed and agreed with the customer:

  - physical dimensions, identifying space limitations for installing components;

o weight of finished item with associated penalties;
o operating parameters; start-up, continuous running, maximum conditions;
o life expected under defined operating conditions;
o specific requirements critical to performance; for example, high temperature;
o mechanical mountings for installation;
o integrate/interface with other systems and subsystems;
o electric and hydraulic connections and interfaces;
o performance parameters in service;
o test parameters to demonstrate design integrity;
o service life under normal operation;
o warranty periods and conditions;
o environmental requirements for the product and processes used in manufacture;
o surface finishes for protection and appearance;
o range of applications and products being replaced;
o special characteristics.

- Potential technical hazards and risks;
- Technical feasibility, through constructing mathematical and physical models;
- Initial concept design studies that identify the operating principles;
- Schematic designs confirming the viability of design concepts;
- Physical models showing critical design features;
- Performance of demonstrators that establish how the product will function;
- Manufacturing processes identified and selected for critical items;
- Initial make vs buy evaluation to determine the supply-chain policy;
- Locations for sourcing core and non-core components;
- Logistics for the supply of component and distribution of products;
- Product costs, based upon building cost estimates at various volume levels, reflecting the experience curve and possible investments in new machinery;
- Product development and non-recurring expenditure needed to acquire the product and manufacturing technology;
- Manufacturing investment in facilities, machine tools, tooling and test equipment needed to ensure product integrity and the installation of additional capacity;

- Product launch costs needed to qualify the unit and the providing of customer evaluation units for gaining technical and quality approvals;
- Supplier assessment to identify sources and prices of non-core components.

Development of the Marketing Approach and Options

- Evaluate the theme for the product and the potential for expanding into other applications;
- Construct the marketing policy, evaluating the component vs system vs product opportunities;
- Determine the possible routes to market to secure maximum returns;
- Establish a plan for exploiting local and global markets;
- Undertake competitor modelling;
- Identify competitor strategies;
- Determine the customer requirements when selecting a supplier:

  o limited technical risk,
  o constraint on funds and cash flow,
  o partnerships on risk and revenue,
  o time to market,
  o need for technology,
  o desire for second source,
  o lower cost solution, and
  o overall reduction in the cost of ownership;

- Identify the decision-makers in the selection process, based upon mapping the influence exerted by members of the customer's decision-making team;
- Seek customer *champions* to provide inside support and guidance;
- Involve contacts throughout the organisation and other influencing groups;
- Identify and select appropriate *red* and *blue* review teams;
- Examine teaming arrangement with competitors and/or allies to provide a more acceptable solution:

  o increase the total package offering a complete solution,
  o represent local/national interests,
  o low-cost source of components,

o risk and revenue sharing,
o acquisition of technology,
o local content and off-set agreements, and
o grants;

- Impact of government policies and the influence of politics:

  o environmental requirements,
  o military funding,
  o purchasing power and policies,
  o need to secure and bolster employment,
  o national strategies,
  o international agreements,
  o reverse trade and off-set agreements on revenue, and
  o legislation and safety standards;

- Bid tactics and the positioning of the company;
- Timing for product launch:

  o meeting the market demand and expectation,
  o introducing new technology ahead of competitors,
  o meeting customers' requirement dates and legal commitments, and
  o catching up with competitors.

Market and Commercial Evaluation

- Confirm the market assumptions:

  o number of units required per year,
  o life of the product in the market,
  o impact on other products – direct substitution, new business or new market segment,
  o aftermarket policies and ownership of business,
  o launch date to meet the market demand,
  o the initial pricing agreement and assumptions,
  o position in the supply chain,
  o the prime customer's position and influence in the market,
  o potential customers and opportunities for expanding the market,
  o understanding of the customer's requirements,
  o route to market,
  o attractiveness of national and international territories, and
  o customer support and aftermarket requirements;

- Determine the pricing policy from a customer (value) and supplier (cost) aspect;
- Construct a high and low sales forecast to be used as the basis for investment;
- Prepare a time-phased profit plan, demonstrating an adequate internal rate of return on investment;
- Identify risks and opportunities, quantifying the impact upon the project;
- Understand the legal commitment and penalties from accepting the contract;
- Establish a marketing plan that identifies the commitments required by the customer;
- Prepare a time phased project plan identifying:

  o objectives and deliverables for the project,
  o work packages needed to undertake and complete the product and process development,
  o key milestones with review dates,
  o work package owners,
  o dates for completing work packages,
  o resources and skills needed for completing work packages,
  o expenditure – capital and revenue, and
  o hazard criteria for escalating problems;

- Estimate the cash flow over the life span of the product;
- Break-even point for the project, and the time before the accumulated cash flow becomes positive.

Preparation of Business Case

The relevant aspects of the detailed analysis needs to be summarised and presented in a concise product business plan. This plan is then presented to a nominated group of senior managers with the authority to sanction the project, supporting the preparation of a bid proposal outlining the necessary customer commitments.

The product business plan must include an objective review of:

- The marketing assumptions used to construct the business case;
- Quantified potential risks and opportunities to the project, covering the market, technology, competitors, commercial, legal and supply-chain issues;

- Target costs based upon the different volume levels, making assessments of possible cost reductions obtained from the experience curve, capital investment, capacity utilisation and sourcing in low-cost territories;
- Pricing strategy, achieving a balance between the customer's perceived value and the supply chain's cost base;
- Investment in product introduction, tooling, plant and equipment, and possible new facilities;
- Competitor evaluation, identifying actions that may be taken in retaliation;
- Overall market assessment related to price and volume, including examining competitor positioning as the market grows to maturity;
- Sales forecast that examines the opportunities for increasing volumes, and the quantified risks associated with the programme;
- Profit forecast with calculated internal rates of return that meet the company objectives;
- Cash flow projection over the life-span of the programme, showing the time taken to achieve a positive cash flow;
- Marketing plan detailing the customers' requirements, and commitments made to exploit the full potential;
- A time-phased project plan showing the key milestones, and an assessment of the manpower resources needed to complete the full product introduction process.

The business case must also be supported with a draft bid proposal that includes a precise summary of the following information:

- A product plan defining:

   o a product design specification with operating parameters,
   o areas requiring development or technology acquisition, and
   o validation procedures and parameters needed to confirm the robustness of the design;

- The status of existing products using similar technologies, and the opportunity for customisation and performance enhancement;
- A statement of the company's responsibilities within the terms of the agreement:

   o the key milestones and deliverables,
   o costs associated with acquiring the capability, and
   o time-scales for delivering units for evaluation, test and production;

- A formal legal development contract (where appropriate);
- A price-and-delivery statement based upon projected volumes;
- A sales/supply contract embodying the company's term and conditions.

Following the formal review, the project is formally signed off with a clear decision on how to proceed. If the outcome is to make *no bid*, based upon an unacceptable level of commercial or technical risk, then this decision must be conveyed to the customer, at the appropriate level, in order to maintain satisfactory future working relationships. Taking a decision to not bid is more difficult than allowing the project to continue. However, the resources available capable of preparing bids and undertaking the subsequent commercial and technical activities are usually over-committed. It is important that the business management team takes responsibility for deciding the business direction, and focusing effort towards winning those programmes that are strategically important to the company. If the business plan is accepted and the decision is to proceed, then the next phase is to prepare a formal customer proposal.

BID PREPARATION

If the decision is to proceed with making a bid, then the marketing team's efforts must be focused towards obtaining a preferred-supplier status, and setting the framework on how to structure the proposal. The task is to deploy all the resources both within and outside the company that can influence the decision-makers into accepting the company's offer. This depends upon gaining a thorough understanding of the customer's overall requirements and integrating them into an acceptable commercial package. All bids are subject to some form of competition, and therefore it is essential to assimilate and analyse the approach that the major competitors will adopt. Establishing red-team/blue-team reviews provides an initial perspective on how companies may respond, but this needs to be supported by informed intelligence concerning the strategies most likely to be adopted.

The preparation of the bid to the customer is the responsibility of the commercial/marketing group and normally requires a direct involvement from the business general manager. The information for preparing the bid should be available from the work undertaken by the project team, and they must also be involved in assessing and agreeing the proposal (see Figure 3.6).

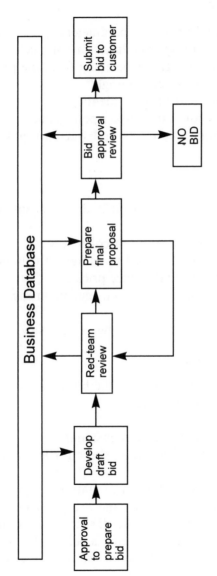

Figure 3.6 Phase 4: preparation of bid proposal ⟶ bid submission

The actual bid submission that is presented to the customer must include relevant clauses covering the following areas:

- *Product definition:*

  o specification and operating parameters;
  o design status and responsibilities for core technologies;
  o intellectual property rights resulting from the project;
  o ownership of patents or copyright;
  o branding policy and product identity;
  o product service and aftermarket policy; and
  o in-service quality guarantees and warranty policies and procedures.

- *Cost and prices:*

  o non-recurring costs for product development, tooling, prototypes and so on;
  o cost recoveries and method of collection;
  o cost and pricing data, based upon agreed volumes;
  o original equipment and service prices;
  o price escalation based upon movements in raw material prices; and
  o currency movement and exchange rate policy.

- *Terms and conditions:*

  o volumes and relative share of the business;
  o terms and condition of sales;
  o payment terms;
  o contract duration and extensions; and
  o cancellation clauses and recompense for loss of contract.

(The company should establish a quotation template that identifies the *ideal, preferred, non-preferred* and *exceptional* options.)

The timing of bid proposals are dictated by customer requests or competition, and therefore the time available for submitting a bid may be relatively short. All bid proposals must be subject to an approval procedure that reflects the importance of the project and the financial risk that the company is taking. Where the quotation to the customer is based upon indicative information regarding the specification, design, volumes, timing or costs, then prices must also be qualified as being tentative and subject to confirmation following subsequent design, development and validation stages. Therefore an important requirement for the business is to establish an internal review mechanism, using the *project classification* to determine the relative importance and risks associated with different projects.

The classification of a project affects:

- Levels of approval and authorisation required to submit a proposal;
- Organisation and project management needed to support the project;
- Reporting structure and the mechanisms required to control the project;
- The hazard criteria and recovery mechanisms; and
- Internal visibility of the project and senior management involvement.

Project Classification – Business Assessment

Four classifications are normally sufficient for distinguishing between the different levels of importance of projects to the business, and the degrees of risk:

Class 1 Projects that have been included in the business plan and are of strategic importance to the company.

Class 1 projects are confirmed by the managing director and the programme office. The business general manager or the programme office can also elevate a class 2 project if it is considered to pose a high risk for the business.

Class 2 Projects included in the business plan that are very important to the business, but do not pose a high commercial or technical risk for the company .

Class 2 projects are confirmed by the business general manager and the programme office. Class 3 projects can be elevated to class 2 by the business general manager or the programme office based upon specific circumstances or potential identified risks.

Class 3 All other projects included in the business plan.

Class 4 Other projects.

Table 3.2 *Classification of a project*

Company classification strategic importance/ risk to company	Business classification value/risk to business		
	high	*medium*	*low*
High	1	2	3
Medium	2	3	4

When confirming the class of a project, it must be examined in respect to the importance and risk it poses to the future of the overall company, and the impact it could have upon a particular business. This classification is then used to determine the level of agreement and authority needed prior to submitting the bid to the customer (see Table 3.2). The basis of company approval should be a formal internal document that is signed off at different levels within the business, depending upon the assigned project classification. This document then provides the authority to submit the bid within agreed financial and technical parameters.

The information presented for authorisation summarises the current position for a project using a consistent format, allowing direct comparisons to be made on the major investment requests from different areas of the company. These can then be reviewed and assessed by the managing director and when necessary approved by the board of directors.

The information that needs to be collated for submitting a bid for approval, allowing a proposal to be made to the customer, is shown in Table 3.3. This internal approval documentation and details of the actual bid are then presented to a *bid approval review* attended by a group of senior managers and directors with the appropriate level of authority to commit expenditure on the project. This is an important management decision point because if the bid is made and accepted, the company is legally committed to undertaking the necessary product developments and meeting the cost targets agreed within the terms of the contract. The review group must take the decision on how to proceed, giving clear instructions on the latitude that can be used in the negotiating process, before having to refer the bid back for further approval. If the outcome is to *not bid*, then careful consideration is needed on the tactics to be adopted when informing

Table 3.3 *Project summary information and status, needed for* Approval to Bid

Project details	All classes of project
Technical specification	Main features confirmed, final detail to be agreed
Operating parameters	Critical working envelope identified with targets
Cost of development	Indicative cost established
Capital investment	Identified against different volume requirements
Initial product cost	Cost of units estimated
Target product cost	Target established based on volume/investment
Delivery milestones	Launch plan detailed
Volume in contract	Planning volumes and level of sales identified
Additional volume	Opportunities for additional sales verified
Share of business	Forecast
Development plan	Developed with resources and time scales
Prototypes	Prices established and order quantities identified
Co-manufactures	Plans confirmed
Partners	Agreement formalised

Financial analysis	
Profit impact	Confirmed by finance manager
Cash flow	Confirmed and source of funds identified
Key business ratios	Acceptable and meet the business criteria
Grants/funding	Identified and agreed in principle
Internal rate of return	Within company targets

Authority levels	*Class 1*	*Class 2*	*Class 3*	*Class 4*
Managing Director	Mandated	As appropriate		
General manager	Mandated	Mandated	Mandated	
Project manager	Mandated	Mandated	Mandated	Mandated

the customer. Customers want a number of alternative proposals, allowing a degree of flexibility when negotiating the terms of the contract so it is important that the company's bid is not used as the mechanism for destroying the market price structure. It must be remembered that business survival depends upon a company winning new contracts, but taking the wrong contract or over-stretching resources can be more damaging than losing a marginal project requiring significant investment and risk.

WINNING THE CONTRACT

Once approved, the bid can be submitted to the customer. The marketing team's effort must focus upon the tactics for submitting the bid and winning the contract. The business team's final position needs to be evaluated and refined into a plan of attack, based upon an in-depth current understanding of competitor's activity. This requires the careful design of messages and calculated responses to manoeuvre the proposal through the correct channels, making all the people in the decision-making loop fully aware of the attractiveness of the proposal and extending support. It must be remembered that people able to influence the choice of supplier often have different criteria, and techniques based upon mapping the decision-making process can provide the spectrum of views needed to structure a winning bid (see Figure 3.7).

The bid proposal must be developed to satisfy the customer's requirements. Submitting the bid usually triggers several iterations of negotiation and amended offers before reaching an agreement that finally wins the bid, leading to an acceptable contract. Throughout the negotiation it is important that the team involved in presenting the proposal:

- manages the bid, including the customer's expectations and the coordination of business contact throughout the period of negotiations;
- understands the customer's overall requirements and the value that is placed upon the different aspects of the proposal, allowing beneficial trade-off to be sought;
- identifies the decision-making group and the criteria that are important to the different parties, leading to a collective assessment of the critical issues and how they will be resolved;
- understands the customer's decision-making process and how this can be influenced to win; and
- anticipates competitor's responses and their reactions after the contract has been awarded.

Throughout the negotiation it is essential to safeguard long term relationships with the customer, irrespective of the final outcome. Therefore, in order to establish good working relationships and build a foundation for future opportunities the team should be aware of:

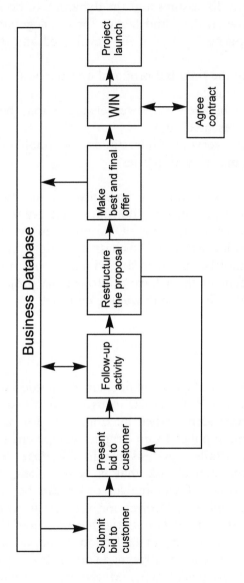

Figure 3.7 Phase 5: submission of bid ——→ win the contract

- Identifying opportunities and importance of win–win situations;
- Selecting the appropriate team of negotiators;
- Creating and controlling the negotiating environment;
- Managing team discussions and the dynamics of decision-taking;
- Establishing the strategy and tactics for the negotiation ensuring the various options have been fully evaluated and the game-plan agreed;
- Understanding the final bid proposal and the best alternative to a negotiated contract;
- Managing the balance of power ensuring that both sides are adequately represented; and
- Ensuring that everyone understands the final agreement and commitments made by all parties.

Contract negotiation requires a specialist set of skills and much depends upon the personal relationships that are established and nurtured often over several years. Obtaining new contracts is probably the most critical aspect of business, because without customers the business cannot be sustained as a viable proposition. Therefore, once the management team have approved the project every conceivable effort must be made to *win* the contract

SUMMARY

This chapter has identified the main elements needed to progress an opportunity into a contract. It has focused upon the internal factors that should be considered when making a bid for new work as a major component supplier to an original equipment manufacturer. The amount of detailed analysis required is dependent upon the technical and commercial risk that is being taken, and in many instances the process of winning an order can be simplified and readily accomplished with information that exists within the company. However, in some instances the business may be '*betting the company*' on a new venture or collection of opportunities, and in these instances judgments must be made on the best information that is available at a particular time. Marketing information is never precise, but intelligent estimates provide a far superior basis for making decisions than a traditional 'gut feel'. The customer development process can consume a disproportional amount of technical and supply-chain resources with little or no returns. Therefore it relies on the management team having the resolve to focus resources onto winning those contracts that meet the strategies agreed in the company's business plan, and which the business has a realistic chance of winning. Taking contracts without this type of prior investment evaluating the commercial and technical risk can result in ill-conceived projects that ultimately ruin the business.

4

Product Introduction Process

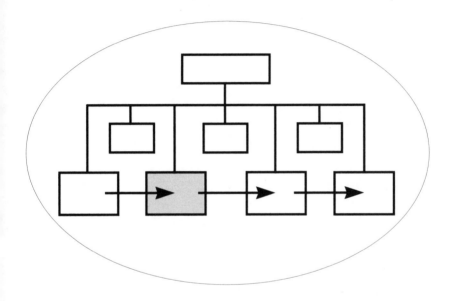

Topics

Introduction
Technology route map
Product introduction plan
Product introduction resources
Project classification
A generic product introduction process
Product and process design
Concept validation
Process implementation
Manufacturing support
Project management
Summary

4

Product Introduction Process

INTRODUCTION

The introduction of new products is crucial to the long-term viability of a company. Once an order has been accepted it is important to have a defined product introduction process that progresses the work carried out in preparing the product specification, through product and process design, and into production. Creating a generic product introduction process that satisfies all sections of manufacturing industry would be far too complex for some particular sectors, but all new product developments must pass through a number of phases. This chapter provides a framework for these processes and identifies the transfer reviews that are required to maintain control, ensuring the project remains on time and within budget.

All new product development projects should be owned by a project manager responsible for driving the day-to-day activities, maintaining schedules, and controlling the budget. The manager must ensure projects follow an agreed procedure, insisting that the technical and quality integrity of the product is not compromised under any circumstances. Further project management tasks are to identify the skill-base needed to advance products from opportunity evaluation through into volume production, and determine which emerging technologies could impact the business, ensuring they are adequately researched and available in time to meet the market demand.

TECHNOLOGY ROUTE MAP

The mechanism for determining a relevant future technical programme is through developing a technology route map. This technique uses the market demand to establish the key technical innovations that will impact the market. The map is constructed as

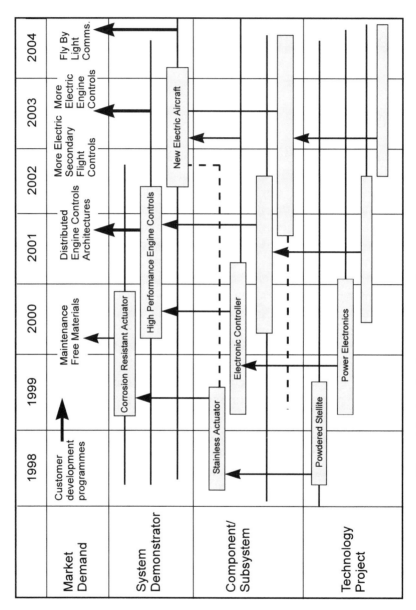

Figure 4.1 A technology route map for aerospace components

a matrix, with dates when the new technologies need to be available for the market plotted horizontally; and the development phases that must be undertaken to bring the product to market– that is, product demonstrator, component or subsystem, basic technologies – plotted vertically. A technology route map can be constructed for most businesses but requires the combined efforts of the management team. The market analysis and prospective customer development programmes provide an informed view of market expectations, but these must be linked to the research programmes being undertaken in universities and laboratories around the world. A judgment is then required to determine which emerging technologies may be applicable, and the innovation needed to create viable, marketable products. This broad review of technology in association with the market requirements is crucial, because in today's rapidly changing technical environment a complete business may be destroyed through not having access to an appropriate technology at the right time.

As an example, a simplified version of a technology route map for aerospace components is shown in Figure 4.1. This should be populated with a number of information blocks describing the development activity, principal participants/collaborators, project status and funding requirements. One such block is shown in more detail in Figure 4.2. The length of the line represents the time frame, with connecting arrows indicating the technology path. This technique is a visual way of highlighting the key technical requirements, the level of technology interdependence, and the time frames available to ensure new products are released on time to meet the market demand.

The development of new products in many industries is being undertaken in collaboration with other companies. Therefore, not all the new technology needs to be developed in-house, but it is essential

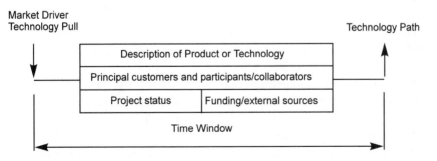

Figure 4.2 An information block for the technology route map

to identify which core technologies the business must retain and invest in if it is to secure a dominant business presence. These basic technologies may be referred to as generic, but are only one aspect of the overall new product introduction requirements.

PRODUCT INTRODUCTION PLAN

The next phase of the product introduction process is to translate the market requirement identified for prospective development projects, opportunity evaluation projects, confirmed product introduction projects and generic technology requirements into an overall *product plan*. This technique structures business opportunities into a product introduction plan which identifies the customer, name of the programme or product, components and subsystems to be supplied, dates for key milestones, and potential value of sales available to the company. The chart (Table 4.1) scopes the level of realistic market opportunities, and the commitments made to major customers for developing new products.

More detailed product plans can be prepared, providing details for all key programme milestones agreed with the customer. These could include:

- Requests for demonstrators;
- Selection of technology concepts;
- Requests for development-phase quotation;
- Completion of first prototype;
- Product selection;
- Requests for production phase quotation;
- First production release;
- Product launch and ramp up production.

Therefore the product plan provides a summary of the main business opportunities and the potential sales revenue that could be obtained from winning contracts. These projects then have to be critically reviewed by the management team to identify those projects that need support with funds and inclusion on the project resource plan. The overall level of resources and funds that will be needed to meet the demands made upon the engineering and production departments to support the opportunity-evaluation and product introduction programmes can then be calculated.

Table 4.1 *Example product plan*

| Customer | Programme | Work content | Bid | Key dates and milestones | | | Sales value |
				Start date	Prototype	Supply	
Generic technology							
Aircar	C YYY	Stainless actuators	Aug. 1997	Jan. 1998	Aug. 2000	Nov. 2001	£23m
Prospective developments							
Aircar	A 390	Undercarriage	Nov. 1997	Mar. 1998	Jan. 2000	Aug. 2002	£15m
Opportunity evaluation							
Firm contracts							

PRODUCT INTRODUCTION RESOURCES

Assessing the number of hours required to complete the full range of
projects comprising the overall technical department workload including *opportunity evaluation* is a necessary but time-consuming
task. The total commitments cover various activities including:

- generic technology,
- new product development,
- new applications of existing products,
- current product enhancement,
- problem resolution and service support,
- improvement projects for cost reduction, and
- engineering services for testing, publications and so on.

The cost estimates prepared must include resources needed for both
product and process development.

   This list appears exhaustive, but all the categories have to be
considered with appropriate costs, in order to obtain an accurate
assessment of the overall product introduction resource requirements. A chart should be generated, by category, providing details
on:

- Name of programme
- Status: whether committed (C), or as a proposal (P) to evaluate
  opportunities
- Project details, by year, over period of the plan

  ○ planned expenditure
  ○ % funded from outside the company
  ○ number of full-time people allocated to project
  ○ resources needed from part-time staff
  ○ major expenditure for capital equipment, tooling and so on
  ○ expenditure on prototypes and consultants

- Source of funding outside the company
- Main customers

Compiling this information requires considerable effort, but it is
important to establish the level of expenditure that is being committed to product introduction programmes, with the management
team taking the decision on the overall budget. They must also

Table 4.2 Product introduction resources requirements

Classification	Programme	Status	1998 £m	1998 % fund	1999 £m	1999 % fund	2000 £m	2000 % fund	Customer/funding source
	Generic Technology								
1	High-power electronics	C	0.6	25	0.9	25	0.5	25	Aircar/DTT
3	Corrosion-resistant material	P	0.3	40	0.4	40	1.2	20	MON
2	Smart controllers	C							
	Other projects								
	Sub-total								
	Product development								
3	Light weight undercarriage	C	0.7	20	0.8	25	1.4	20	Moeing/DTI
1	Smart engine control	P	0.4	0	0.6	0	0	0	S E
	Other projects								
	Sub-total								
	New Applications								
1	M-888 Primary flight controls	C	1.0	30	1.2	30.	0.4	30	Moeing
	A-377 undercarriage	C	0.6	20	0.4	20	0.6	20	Aircar
	Other projects								
	Sub-total								
	Product Enhancement								
	S E Military engine control								
	Other projects								
	Sub-total								
	Problem Resolution								
	Sub-total								
	Improvement Projects								
	Sub-total								
	Engineering Services								
	Sub-total								
	Total committed								
	Total								

identify which projects take priority and direct finite resources to the area of greatest value for the company. An example is shown in Table 4.2.

This table needs to be supported by additional information derived from a more detailed analysis of the project resource requirement, defining people allocated to the project (on both a full and part-time basis), and the level of capital investment in manufacturing hardware and test facilities. This information is also needed to support the project approval procedures and the project management system.

PROJECT CLASSIFICATION

All product introduction projects contain an element of both financial and technical risk. A procedure has been identified within the customer development process that allows projects to be systematically assessed to determine their level of commercial risk and relative importance to the business, providing guidance on where to focus management attention. These assessment tools need to be tailored to specific types of businesses, but the elements identified in the previous chapter provide a basis for an effective scoring system. The relative importance of these factors can only be determined by the management team, and requires subjective judgment based upon the critical factors that directly impact the business.

All projects will have been assigned a classification from the *opportunity evaluation* stage, and this should be reassessed to confirm a project's classification at the start of the product introduction process. A project's classification determines the level of authorisation and visibility required by senior managers. In most cases *four categories* of project give sufficient differentiation between the various types of project. The project classification signifies the relative commercial risk associated with a project and rules should have been established to identify how each class of project will be authorised and controlled:

Class 1   Projects *strategically important* to the future of the *company*, or classification 2 projects elevated to classification 1 based upon their importance to a business.

Class 2   Projects *important* to the *business*, or classification 3 projects elevated to classification 2 by the general manager based upon their strategic impact for the business.

Class 3   Projects of *high importance* to a *product family* or, classification 4 projects elevated to classification 3 based upon their risk to the business.

Class 4   All other projects.

The higher the classification, the more management attention is needed in assessing the commercial benefits and supporting the project as it progresses through the various stages.

A GENERIC PRODUCT INTRODUCTION PROCESS

The product introduction process is one of the key business processes. It encompasses all the activities necessary to progress a new product from winning a development order from the customer, or obtaining management commitment to develop a product, through to releasing the product for manufacture. The activities prior to this stage are contained within the *customer development process*. However, these two processes have to be integrated, changing emphasis from commercial and technical evaluation to creating a product that exceeds the customer's expectations. A product introduction process has two main elements; product and process development, and programme management. It is based upon four interrelated phases that can be defined as:

- Product and process design and development;
- Concept validation;
- Process implementation and verification; and
- Manufacturing support.

Each phase has to be supported by a specification of the product and process requirements, a formal review procedure, and the application of recommended *tools* to ensure all critical aspects for a project have been considered and resolved (see Figure 4.3).

The process is managed by a series of formal technical and commercial reviews that checks the progress at specific stages of the project, and is supported by a management approval mechanism that authorises continuation to the next phase. The review examines all the relevant business, technical and project management issues. To be successful, the product introduction management process has to be structured around three critical items that support the two main

106

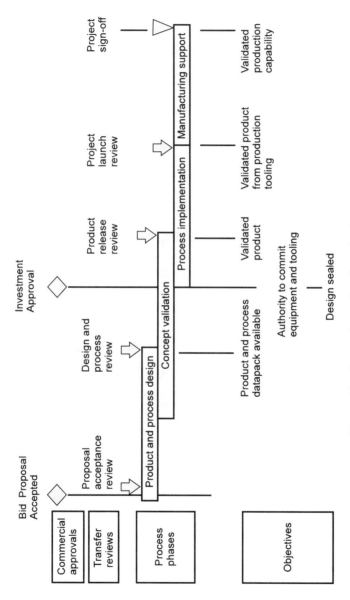

Figure 4.3 A generic product introduction process

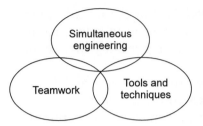

Figure 4.4   Three factors integrated by the product introduction process

elements of *product and process development,* and *project management.* This involves creating an environment for innovation, and integrating the three factors shown in Figure 4.4.

Simultaneous Engineering

The purpose of simultaneous engineering is to establish concurrent activities, ensuring that product and manufacturing processes are designed and developed in parallel. It also requires suppliers and customers to be actively involved in the product introduction process, integrating them into the activities at the earliest opportunity. This means seeking their participation in the day-to-day work of the project teams, the project planning process, and attendance at all project reviews.

Team Working

The 'team work' philosophy is aimed at developing a multidisciplinary core of people, controlled by a project manager to take overall responsibility for progressing the project from opportunity evaluation through to manufacturing support. For class 1 and 2 projects this means:

- Assigning a full time project manager to the project;
- Identifying multidisciplinary and multifunctional team members;
- Allocating full-time core members to the team;
- Assigning the part-time resources needed by the team;
- Co-locating the project team into a designated area, equipped with appropriate engineering data management and CAD/CAM systems;
- Assembling the project team at the start of the project;

- Involving all members of the team in preparing the project plan and obtaining commitment to delivering the key milestones;
- Providing team training leading to a common understanding for team members;
- Authorising the project manager and team to control expenditure within the approved project budget;
- Selecting the team members, considering the team's strengths and weaknesses; and
- Considering the career development needs of team members.

The introduction of effective team working means that the demands of the hierarchical and functionally-driven organisation must be replaced with a commitment to teams, focused towards meeting the customers' needs, using a product introduction process controlled by a project manager.

Tools and Techniques

Tools and techniques used in the product introduction process have continued to evolve over the past decade, and should be applied whenever appropriate throughout the project. The four most commonly used techniques are as follows:

Quality Function Deployment (QFD)

Quality function deployment is a structured, analytical technique developed to accurately capture the customers' requirements, translating them into key product features to be incorporated effectively into the product design.

The process uses a chart-based system that structures the customer's requirements into relevant marketing, design and supply-chain information. The technique begins with establishing external requirements and progressively grouping these into more focused objectives. The *customer's needs* are translated into the *top-level design requirements* through grouping the customer *wants* into primary, secondary and tertiary parameters, and identifying *how* these features can be incorporated into the design. The value of the chart increases as more information is progressively added. The completed chart containing all the relevant information on the market, product and process-design interface is known as QFD 1. Additional charts are generated in a similar way for:

QFD 2   Interface between *concept design* and *detailed design*
QFD 3   Interface between *detailed design* and *manufacturing processes*
QFD 4   Interface between *manufacturing processes* and *production methods*

The QFD technique:

- Provides a stronger customer focus;
- Results in fewer changes to the design and identifies them earlier in the process;
- Promotes multifunctional team-working and stimulation of ideas;
- Reduces the development time by removing the need for excessive iterations;
- Improves communication and promotes a common understanding of objectives;
- Reduces non-recurring project costs due to the elimination of misinterpretations and iterations;
- Provides clarity on the customer's requirements at every stage of the process;
- Results in fewer problems at later stages of the product introduction process when modifications are considerably more expensive to introduce; and
- Provides a competitive edge due to the intrinsic encapsulation of market requirements.

Design for Assembly (DFA)

Design for assembly is a tool that improves the design of both the product and the assembly process by forcing the creation of a design that is fundamentally simpler in construction and inherently simpler to assemble (and dis-assemble), without compromising the desired functionality. The process is based upon three stages:

- *Functional analysis* – how essential is it for a part to be a separate item? Examining ways of combining several elements into a single part.
- *Handling analysis* – examines how easy it is to handle a part; that is, picking it up and orientating it ready for assembly. Each aspect is scored depending upon its complexity, and a handling ratio established allowing a direct comparison of design solutions.

- *Fitting analysis* – evaluating the ease of holding and fitting the part into the assembly. An assembly sequence flow chart is compiled, and each activity in the process assigned a cost index that again allows the comparison of designs.

Some of the benefits derived from applying the process include:

- reduced parts count;
- lower component and assembly costs;
- reduced time to market due to improved design and assembly processes;
- improved product quality and reliability; and
- a structured process for evaluating the critical features of different designs.

Failure Mode and Effects Analysis (FMEA)

The purpose of the *product* FMEA is to root out the elements in the *concept design* that could cause product failure. The product and components are examined by a group of people who identify and record the function, failure mode and mechanism, means of detection and their effects at the local module and higher equipment levels.

The purpose of the *process* FMEA is to root out the areas in the *component design* and *production processes* that are likely to fail or significantly impair the production processes.

Benefits from employing the design and process FMEAs include:

- increased equipment reliability, based upon higher integrity components;
- reduced development time due to the elimination of design and process weaknesses;
- improved production efficiency due to more robust manufacturing processes; and
- lower overall project costs and cost of ownership due to the prevention of failures.

Design of Experiments (DOE)

Design of experiments is based upon using statistical methods to control and limit the number of experiments needed to establish and predict the trends and impact on product, or production performance, due to changes in key parameters. Benefits from the technique include:

- reduced costs due to the elimination of non-value-added experimentation;
- shorter lead-times for releasing products into the market; and
- improved products and processes that perform consistently and are more robust due to the elimination of variability.

PRODUCT AND PROCESS DESIGN

The first stage of the process is to confirm the technical specification and review concept product design and process solutions, prepared as part of the opportunity evaluation. Further design studies are then required that analyse and refine the concepts to a level that can be manufactured and tested. The work should be performed by a multidisciplinary team with the necessary skill-base needed to complete the tasks, working directly for a project manager responsible for managing day-to-day activities, controlling the budget, and striving to meet the agreed milestones. Full involvement of the customer and suppliers should be sought and encouraged throughout this phase of the project, to ensure the preferred design solution provides the lowest cost of ownership, and meets all the functional requirements of the application (see Figure 4.5).

The first review after winning the bid is the *proposal acceptance review*. This should be a mandatory meeting called and chaired by the general manager for all class 1 and 2 projects. Other team members expected to attend this and subsequent project reviews are:

- Project director;
- Customer satisfaction director;
- Finance director;
- Project manager of the project;
- Selected project team members;
- Functional heads from:

  o quality,
  o engineering,
  o sales and marketing,
  o manufacturing,
  o purchasing, and
  o distribution and aftermarket;

112

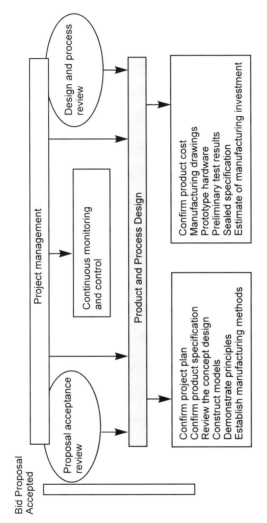

Figure 4.5 Product and process design

- Customers;
- Key suppliers;
- Partners and co-makers.

Projects with a lower classification should be subject to a similar review chaired by the project director and attended by appropriate department managers, depending on the status of the project. If the project fails to meet its key milestone commitments, then the project director elevates the project classification and insists that the managers accountable for commercial and technical integrity attend and agree the recovery programme.

The proposal acceptance review is held immediately an order or agreement of understanding is received from the customer or, for internally sponsored projects, from the managing director. A standard format and reporting procedure should be adopted for each review including a formal sign-off and acceptance sheet summarising the recommendations of the meeting and providing authorisation for proceeding to the next phase.

Checklist of Items to be Presented at the Proposal Acceptance Review

Business Appraisal

- Proposal response including:

  o variations to the proposal presented at the *submit bid to the customer* review;
  o terms and conditions, including the pricing policy;
  o time-scales for the key milestones;
  o product quantities required for evaluation, prototypes and production;
  o other project deliverables and commitments; and
  o a valid time of agreement.

- Business acceptance including:

  o resource availability and summary of the skills required;
  o capacity availability on equipment and facilities;
  o changes in strategy/policy for the proposed product range; and
  o changes in trading conditions.

- Market factors including:

  o changes in the marketplace;
  o changes in national economies where the product is to be sold; and
  o technologies and substitute products that could provide an alternative solution.

Technical Appraisal

- Proposal response including:

  o modifications to approved proposal;
  o design-concept review and appraisal of areas needing development; and
  o evaluation of technologies including an assessment of innovation.

- Status of the technical specification.
- Target cost evaluation against preliminary cost estimates and feasibility confirmed.

Programme and Project Management

- Project costs – estimated and budgets agreed, funding established.
- Resources – skills needed identified, availability checked against the master project plan.
- Project plan – confirmed as feasible, customer/project milestones established, and time-scales fit with overall commitments.
- Project specification – clearly defined terms of reference, detailed project specification, target project costs, assessed level of risk, and defined project classification.
- Project organisation – project manager appointed.

Once the proposal acceptance review summary report has been formally signed off by the business general manager and the project director, the project is officially launched. This signals the start of the product introduction process which begins by assembling the full-time team committed to the project. The first phase is the *product and process design*, and work is focused towards transforming the items listed in Table 4.3 under *start* into *deliverables*.

Table 4.3 *Details of the product and process design phase*

Start $\longrightarrow$	Deliverables
Business plan approved by management team	Product design defined and documented
Outline project plan	Manufacturing process selected
Multifunctional team appointed	Make vs buy strategy agreed
Involvement from aftermarket and distribution	Manufacturing locations identified
Partners and key suppliers involved	Preliminary test results – confirmed integrity
Customer requirements understood and accepted	Manufacturing investments calculated
	Manufacturing system documented
Technical performance specification agreed	Bill of materials available
Appropriate design tools identified	Failure mode effects analysis compiled
Environmental legislation requirement known	Quality plan documented
Patent searches begun	Critical parts identified
Concept designs available for review	Patent applications prepared
Initial performance analysis completed	Reliability and maintenance schemes drafted
Concept models available	Reliability calculations initiated
Preliminary evaluation and test results obtained	
Manufacturing processes identified established	Make vs buy defined
	Sources identified
Test and qualification parameters agreed	Customer requirements confirmed
Regulatory requirements understood	Changes to contract negotiated
	Technical changes to specification agreed
Customer commitment obtained	Number of changes requests documented
Commercial contract negotiated	
Responsibilities and liabilities confirmed	
Aftermarket terms agreed	
Manufacturing investment accepted	
Price, volumes and delivery dates confirmed	
Project profitability accepted by company	
Expenditures on non-recurring items budgeted	
Target costs tabled	
Customer milestones known	
Delivery dates accepted for prototypes	
Launch delivery dates known	
Ramp-up volumes agreed	
Marketing development plans	

Tools and Techniques Recommended for this Product and Process Design Phase

- Quality function deployment confirming the design satisfies the customer's requirements.
- Design of experiment to improve the integrity and robustness of the product and process design.
- Failure mode and effects analysis for the product and process.
- Design of assembly techniques.
- Design to cost.

Depending upon the type of product, other specialist computer-based tools should be used for evaluating dynamic performance, stress analysis, reliability assessments, rapid prototyping, manufacturing systems design, and so on.

When the deliverables outlined above have been accomplished to the satisfaction of the functional heads and project manager, a second review is convened by the general manager together with the other team members, customers and suppliers present at the previous review. This *product and process design review* should again follow a standard format with a formal assessment and sign-off procedure.

Checklist of Items to be Presented at the Product and Process Design Review

Business Appraisal

- Strategic implications – satisfies the business strategy and product policy.
- Marketing plan – target customers aligned, plan defined, business need confirmed.
- Target product costs – target cost verified as achievable, non-recurring costs budgeted.
- Sales forecast – credibility and confidence level determined.
- Investment – capital investment and cash outflow profile agreed, and sanctions for expenditure submitted.
- Commercial – pricing policy defined, unit prices agreed with the customer, customer commitment formally acknowledged.
- Financial model – cash and profit profiles calculated and compared to level of returns expected by the company.
- Risk assessment – commercial, technical, and possible patent infringements completed.

Technical Appraisal

- Proposed product design including:

  o drawings and analysis approved by the responsible design authorities;
  o concept functionally proved by product demonstrators;
  o working tolerances reviewed and accepted;
  o system integration and mounting arrangements agreed;
  o installation drawings complete;
  o bill of materials signed off by the engineering design authority and purchasing;
  o design documentation completed;
  o test and performance specifications agreed and confirmed as viable;
  o impact of the product on the environment evaluated and confirmed as being within legal limits; and
  o QFD, DFA, FMEA and DOE techniques applied to verify the robustness of product and process design.

- Selected manufacturing process including:

  o make vs buy complete to determine items to be manufactured in-house;
  o manufacturing methods documented, and capability requirements of the process confirmed;
  o manufacturing system designed and key plant identified;
  o physical layout of manufacturing routes established;
  o cost of equipment and installation confirmed;
  o product cost at various levels of production and investment verified;
  o process FMEA completed; and
  o preferred suppliers for bought-out items selected and prices negotiated.

- Performance and physical parameters agreed with customer, including:

  o size, weight, mountings, interfaces and installation envelope;
  o operating conditions – speed, temperature, start-up conditions, expected life, operating environment;
  o critical performance requirement and operating features;
  o interfaces – electrical, mechanical, fluids, air.

- Patent searches and new patent drafted in readiness for application.
- Time-scales for demonstration units, prototypes, validation units and production negotiated.
- Reliability testing and techniques for verifying product quality documented.
- Health, safety and environmental requirements of the manufacturing process and substances used in manufacture identified.

Programme and Project Management

- Project costs confirmed and funding agreed.
- Resources identified and availability confirmed.
- Project plan agreed and approved by managers responsible for key deliverables.
- Reporting system with appropriate measures and monitors established.
- Key milestones agreed with the customer and verified as attainable.
- Project specification, objectives, deliverables, classification and levels of authority agreed.
- Project manager and team members dedicated to project.

This list establishes the significant aspects of the project that need to be considered at the review. However, the management team is responsible for approving the project and allowing it to proceed to the next stage. They must identify those items that are most pertinent to the business, and the review must ensure all critical aspects have been adequately evaluated and the business is not exposed to unnecessary or foreseeable risks.

CONCEPT VALIDATION

The validation phase of the project ensures the product performance, reliability and environmental requirements are compliant with the agreed specification. Additional samples may be required for evaluation, but these should be manufactured using the designated production equipment and tooling, making them as similar to final production units as possible. The validation phase and work on the product and process design often run in parallel until the design and process design review is complete. This allows results from the initial tests to be incorporated into the design, making it more robust. The phase ends with a fully validated and quality-approved product that meets the technical specification and satisfies the customer's requirements. The design has also to meet in-house criteria for limiting the exposure to unacceptable commercial risks. The main deliverables from this phase are a final issue information pack that defines a compliant product and associated manufacturing routes. All work is undertaken by a multidisciplinary team under the control of the project manager but the mix of skills and people assigned to the project may change to reflect the tasks being undertaken. Details of this stage are shown in Figure 4.6 and Table 4.4.

Table 4.4 *Details of the concept validation phase*

Start ⟶	Deliverables
Multifunctional team assigned	Validated product
Make vs buy complete	Validated manufacturing process
Preferred suppliers involved	Validated tooling
Customer involved	Compliance to customer specifications
Aftermarket consulted	
	Customer inspection report and
Critical component available for test	assessment
Designated manufacturing processes	Finalised process specification
used	Agreed and approved product
Customer engineering approval obtained	specification
	Signed off manufacturing process
Process routes identified	Documentation – product
Manufacturing facilities identified	Documentation – process
Product specification agreed and	Firm production and test schedules
approved	
Products manufactured to drawing	Confirmed bill of materials
tolerances	Product launch plan
Bill of materials	Production start and volume ramp-up
Quality plan prepared	plans
	Product transition and substitution
Prices of bought-out components	plans
confirmed	Upgraded quality plan controls
Material purchases approved	confirmed
Long lead-time items identified	Training plan for the workforce
Critical items provisionally released	developed
Plant and equipment budget, suppliers	Validated production methods and
contacted	capacity
	Process capability checked
Customer test schedules	
Customer production requirements	

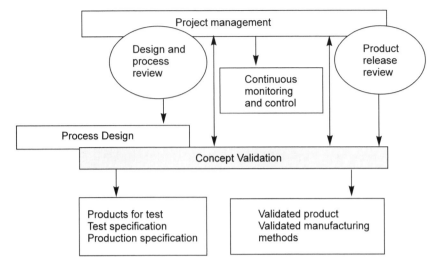

Figure 4.6 Concept validation

Tools and Techniques Recommended for the Concept Validation Phase

- Quality function deployment.
- Design of experiments.
- Failure modes and effects analysis.

When the objectives outlined have been accomplished to the satisfaction of the functional heads and the project manager, a *product release review* is convened by the general manager attended by other members of the management review team, customers and suppliers present at previous reviews.

Checklist of Items to be Presented at the Product Release Review

Business Appraisal

- Strategic implications and fit with product policy.
- Marketing plan with identified target customers, confirmation that the product meets the customer's requirements, and a plan to exploit further opportunities.
- Target product costs, non-recurring costs, recurring costs and actual unit costs.

- Sales forecast based upon firm commitments and level of confidence of prospective sales, for both the original equipment and aftermarket customers.
- Investment in capital equipment, plant and facilities including grants and customers' contributions.
- Commercial planning – pricing strategy, product line profitability, cash-flow and profit projections, risk and volume sensitivity analysis.
- Suppliers and co-makers identified with confirmed prices with agreed liabilities and responsibilities.
- Customer price structure agreed, specification confirmed, with firm delivery dates and production volumes.

Technical Appraisal

- Product, including

  o specification confirmed and signed off by the customer;
  o failure modes for the product and process assessed with appropriate corrective actions;
  o bill of materials signed off by the design authority and purchasing;
  o critical parts evaluated to simplify the design and manufacturing methods verified;
  o production drawings and processing documentation signed off;
  o aftermarket and service requirements documented; and
  o first application inspection report signed off by the customer.

- Manufacturing process, including

  o manufacturing system and production method documented;
  o factory layouts and plans drawn;
  o production routes and detailed cell design in progress;
  o materials handling and the flow of materials established;
  o measuring systems and gauges identified;
  o product verification and test methods developed;
  o machine capabilities checked;
  o manufacturing tolerances reviewed to determine critical inspection features;
  o operating parameters for critical processes confirmed and documented;
  o tooling drawings and tooling policy available;
  o machining fixtures and tool holders designed and priced;

- o assembly techniques developed and support equipment evaluated;
- o production test equipment and conformance verification methods identified;
- o health and safety review complete on all equipment, processes and substances used in the manufacturing process in-house and at suppliers;
- o environmental impact of process, waste materials and recycling of the product documented;
- o packaging for shipment and ease of handling by the customer agreed; and
- o containers required for protection against the environment specified.

- Results of validation tests, including

  - o test results and reports documented;
  - o customer evaluation and acceptance test reports available for review;
  - o critical performance or design weaknesses critically assessed and reported;
  - o final performance specification agreed and signed off by the customer;
  - o results from field trials and endurance tests satisfactory; and
  - o completed verification report on the product and implications for the manufacturing process compiled.

Programme and Project Management

- Project achievements relative to key milestones, costs and delivery promises.
- Review of project funding against plan and the estimated *cost to complete*.
- Summary of results of performance measures used to report and track progress.
- Resource plan – detailing the availability of equipment, and skilled people in relation to the master project plan.
- Project plan confirmed and agreed with the customer for the next stages of the project including recovery plans through to project completion.
- Project specification – confirmed terms of reference, specification and classification.

- Overall project assessment report including a summary of the technical and commercial risks.

This list again includes the significant items that must be considered by the management team prior to allowing the project to proceed. However, it is incumbent upon the review team to identify those items that are critical to the business and confirm that these aspects have been adequately addressed, and in sufficient detail to prevent the company from being commercially exposed.

PROCESS IMPLEMENTATION

This phase of the process is concerned with preparing the production facilities ready for the manufacture of the new product. This includes the purchase of any new plant, reorganising facilities, implementing manufacturing cells and establishing assembly and test areas. Other items that have to be addressed are verifying tooling, materials handling techniques, supply of materials and the provision of operator training. The start of this phase is a *commercial investment appraisal review* that approves the investment needed in the production facilities and releases the expenditure for early production tooling. This phase can start prior to the completion of the validation phase, once the product design has been demonstrated to be robust, able to be manufactured and approved by the customer. At this stage the product design must be firm, requiring only minor amendment and modifications to optimise performance. The deliverable from this phase is *job 1*, which is the first production unit to be delivered to the customer from the fully-functional production unit, using an approved process and tooling (see Figure 4.7).

Investment Approval

This review signifies the start of the *process implementation* phase and the company's commitment to make significant investments in facilities and equipment needed to manufacture the product in volume and at a competitive price. The project can only proceed past this milestone by obtaining full backing from the company to fund and underwrite the investment, and a commitment from the customer to

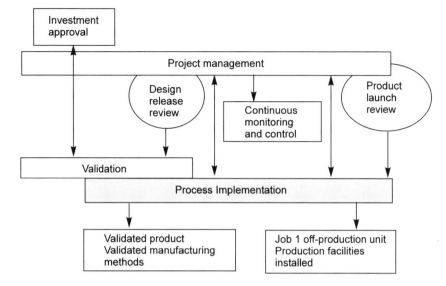

Figure 4.7 Process implementation

place orders for the product. This understanding must be formally documented and is part of the legally binding contract between the two companies.

At this stage the product design is firm, and all subsequent changes must be subject to an approved *engineering change control* procedure; any changes must now be recorded and significant modifications made at the customer's request reflected in a further quotation or adjustment to the agreed price.

The documentation for the *investment appraisal* review is based upon the product business plan prepared for the *proposal to bid* review, using current information and firmer market projections on future demand. The reviews for Class 1 and 2 projects are chaired by the managing director supported by board members and appropriate senior managers. Class 3 and 4 projects are chaired by the business' general manager with the necessary senior management support.

The *product business plan* must be formally presented to include the following commercial and technical information:

- A final customer and marketing plan that identifies the market potential and ways of exploiting the product.
- Latest estimates of costs and prices based upon the production volumes and product maturity.

- Agreed terms and conditions of sale with the lead customer, and firm commitments made to other customers.
- Technical report on the product and process, highlighting any remaining performance gaps against the specification or incapable manufacturing processes.
- Summary of the make vs buy strategy linked to a sourcing plan that is supported with firm prices from committed suppliers.
- Investment plan for facilities, plant and equipment, and tooling.
- Project plan detailing the expenditure to date, and detailed work-packages for the process implementation phase.
- Funding statement on the cost to complete the project.
- Training plan identifying the skills required by the workforce.
- A financial statement that provides profit projections, time-phased cash-flow statements, and a full project assessment against the investment criteria established by the managing director.
- Statement on the funds needed to commence process implementation.

A successful investment appraisal gives the authority to start the implementation process and the seeking of formal approval to purchase capital equipment. The commercial team also proceed with preparing a final contract with the customer. The formal commercial contract should include:

- The final product specification and acceptance criteria, backed by a statement on the current status of the design.
- Statement of the intellectual property, its assignment, patents and copyright.
- Quality standards and compliance to legal requirements.
- Volume commitments and shares of the projected business.
- Recovery of non-recurring costs.
- Ownership and funding of tooling and specialist test equipment.
- Branding and information required for tracing manufacturing details.
- Price structures for original equipment and aftermarket.
- Terms and conditions of sale, including payment periods.
- Price escalation clauses for movement in raw materials prices and exchange rates.
- Duration of the contract and conditions for cancellation.
- Product service policy and in service warranties.
- Cost and pricing statement based upon the projected volumes.

Table 4.5 *Details of process implementation phase*

Start ⟶	Deliverables
Multifunctional team assigned	Validated product from production
Preferred suppliers and co-makers	tooling
involved	Installed validated manufacturing
Customer involved	process
Aftermarket involved	Proved validated tooling
	Capacity availability confirmed
Critical parts and processes documented	
Customer engineering approval signed	Customer initial sample inspection
off	report
Process routes verified with known	Confirmed process specification
capability	Firm product specification
Manufacturing facilities confirmed	Manufacturing process implemented
Product specification firm and approved	Full documentation for the product
Products manufactured to drawing	Full documentation of the process
tolerances	Firm production and test schedules
Bill of materials signed off	Equipment installed and commissioned
Quality plan established and controls	Confirmed bill of materials
agreed	Product launch plan determined
	Production ramp-up schedule confirmed
Prices of bought out components firm	Product transition and substitution
Material purchases approved	planned
Long lead-time items ready for release	Quality plan and controls implemented
Critical items provisionally released	Training plan for the workforce in
Plant and equipment budget, suppliers	progress
identified	
	Process capability of processes known
Customer test schedules agreed	
Customer production requirements	
acknowledged	

The process implementation phase of the project continues in parallel with the commercial negotiation and focuses upon preparing the facilities needed to manufacture the product in the required volumes. Details of this phase are shown in Table 4.5.

Tools and Techniques Recommended for this Phase

- Failure mode and effects analysis for the production process.
- Statistical process control and process capability studies.
- Design of experiments to improve the robustness of the process.
- Preventative maintenance techniques and plant refurbishment.
- Cutting trials and tool-life studies.

Another requirement that must be given full consideration is creating a manufacturing module within the factory, ensuring that the team associated with the product can establish an identity, taking pride in and ownership of the product. The people involved in manufacturing the pre-*job 1* batches should be encouraged to form improvement groups to feed their initial experiences back into the production processes.

Once *job 1* has been produced to the satisfaction of the customer and the functional heads, a *product launch review* is convened by the general manager and attended by other members of the review team, customers and suppliers.

Checklist of Items to be Presented at the Product Launch Review

Business Appraisal

- Marketing plan with confirmed customers' commitments, further established marketing opportunities and the business objectives reconciled with market requirements.
- Target product costs confirmed using the installed manufacturing methods and production tooling. Unit costs based upon the level of investment and expected *learner curves* identified with plans for delivering the expected cost-savings.
- Sales forecast projections based upon firm customer schedules and prospective orders with their respective level of confidence, for both the original equipment and aftermarket sales.
- Commercial planning – pricing confirmed ensuring satisfactory product line profitability, cash flow and profitability confirmed in a full financial analysis, and a sensitivity analysis conducted to illustrate the commercial risks due to changes in volume, selling prices or manufacturing costs.
- Suppliers and co-makers' contracts signed with firm price and delivery commitments.
- Customer price structures agreed, pre-delivery inspection checks confirmed, together with firm delivery dates and production volumes.

Technical Appraisal

- Customer, including:

  o delivery schedules confirmed and accepted as achievable;
  o shipment and packaging details confirmed and evaluated; and

- o samples manufactured using the installed production methods formally approved by the customer and verified by in-house assessment.

- Design release including:

  - o full product definition data-file complete and released to production;
  - o changes from final evaluation trials incorporated into the design documentation;
  - o manufacturing routings and bill of material installed on factory manufacturing planning and control system;
  - o design validation testing including completed customer trials;
  - o development and performance test reports issued;
  - o design review complete with all recommendations implemented;
  - o actions from design FMEA complete;
  - o action from process FMEA complete; and
  - o product specification sealed.

- Manufacturing process definition including:

  - o manufacturing system installed in factory and process-validated;
  - o manufacturing and assembly equipment installed, commissioned and checked for process capability;
  - o tooling, fixtures and materials-handling devices validated after producing significant trial quantities;
  - o final first-off samples checked and verified to drawing instructions;
  - o critical manufacturing features identified and statistical process controls established to monitor key parameters;
  - o assembly process documented and supported with appropriate tooling, fixtures and mechanical handling devices;
  - o test specifications documented, test methods commissioned and validated;
  - o gauging and inspection systems confirmed and checked for process capability;
  - o tool and gauge control systems implemented;
  - o machine preventative maintenance plans developed;
  - o all existing machines transferred to the facility and refurbished prior to installation;
  - o in-process handling and packaging available;
  - o production capacity validated and ways to expand production identified;

- o process specifications confirmed and sealed;
- o manufacturing data-pack finalised and factory documentation released;
- o health, safety and environment controls implemented;
- o bought-out components and materials passed incoming validation and inspection tests; and
- o critical features and inspection sampling plans agreed with materials and component suppliers.

- Training, including:

  - o all operators, craftsmen and assembly and test people trained;
  - o quality and audit people trained; and
  - o specialist training for hazardous processes and controls implemented.

- Manufacturing conformance, including:

  - o critical component features identified and control mechanisms established;
  - o assembly audit procedure documented and implemented;
  - o self-fault diagnostic techniques applied to the production processes;
  - o material traceability and control systems specified;
  - o production quality targets established and agreed; and
  - o quality procedures documented and people trained in their application.

- Production confidence and state of readiness, including:

  - o reject rates achieved on the initial trial production;
  - o scrap and the cost of quality known and targets established;
  - o cycle times for the key bottlenecks that limit overall capacity identified;
  - o corrective actions needed for ensuring full process capability implemented;
  - o tool life on dedicated tooling documented;
  - o change overtimes on equipment and test facilities recorded and plans available for achieving significant reductions;
  - o achievements compared to benchmark performance goals;
  - o procurement schedules confirmed with the status of critical items known;
  - o stock levels and work in progress targets agreed; and

- ○ Lead times for material processing compared to waiting time monitored.
- Continuous improvement including:
  - ○ improvement plans established with full cell team involvement; and
  - ○ management audit procedures documented and implemented.

Programme and Project Management

- Project achievements relative to key milestones and delivery dates summarised.
- Product costs relative to budget, actual and estimated known.
- Review of project funding against plan and estimated cost to complete confirmed.
- Summary of the performance using measures identified to report and track progress.
- Resources requirement plan detailing the skills needed to complete the project and its impact upon the project master plan.
- Project plan agreed with the customer through to the completion of the project.
- Overall project assessment, highlighting areas of risk and the actions taken to minimise potential problems.

This list needs to be reviewed by the management team and all critical items must be completed before signing the formal project summary review report, allowing the project to proceed to the final stage.

MANUFACTURING SUPPORT

This phase is concerned with building up the production output to the volumes needed to meet the customer delivery schedules. The product introduction team remains assigned to the project to resolve any problems that arise with the product or process as manufacturing volumes are increased to meet the specified manufacturing capacity. If the previous phases of the project have been successful, then work in this phase will comprise engineering concessions, adjustments to machining tolerances, tooling modifications, resolving supplier problems and minor modifications. The product introduction management process as envisaged in this chapter will have failed if major changes are needed to the product or process after *job 1*. The other task for the project team is to expand the customer base and obtain

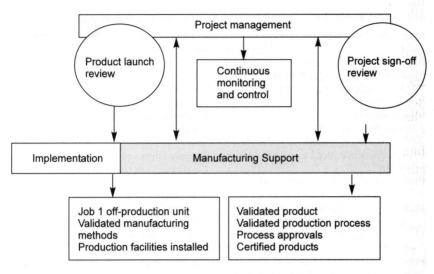

Figure 4.8 Manufacturing support

the certification and approvals needed to supply products. Several products have to be tested by the customer or qualifying authority for conformance to technical specifications, and production methods inspected and approved before commencing deliveries (see Figure 4.8 and Table 4.6).

This phase starts immediately after the product launch review for *job 1*, and finishes with the transfer of responsibilities for the product and process from the project team to operations and engineering support. The deliverable from this phase is a capable, documented, viable production process.

Tools and Techniques Recommended for this Phase

- Failure mode and effects analysis for the production process.
- Statistical process control and process capability studies.

The final review is the project *sign off* signifying *the end* of the project, with responsibility for design and the manufacturing process passing to manufacturing and product support. The project team is formally disbanded and team members assigned to another project. The project *sign-off review* is convened by the general manager and attended by other members of the review team assigned to the project, customers and suppliers.

Table 4.6   *Details of the manufacturing support phase*

Start ———————▶	*Deliverables*
Multifunctional team assigned	Validated product in volume production
Preferred suppliers and co-makers involved	Validated production capacity
Customer involved	Plan for cost reduction identified
Aftermarket involved	Methods of expanding capacity established
Critical parts produced using production tooling	Process approved by customer
Processing parameters confirmed	Confirmed operational process
	Firm product specification
Process routes established with known capability	Manufacturing control system operational
Production facilities installed and commissioned	Full documentation for the product
	Full documentation of the process
Product specification firm and approved	Firm production schedules
Products manufactured using capable processes	Equipment installed and fully capable
Bill of materials signed off	Continuous improvement groups initiated
Quality plan and controls implemented	Lessons learnt documented
	Quality plan and controls operating
Prices of bought-out components firm	Process validated by independent assessment
Materials available for manufacture	Training plan for the workforce complete

Checklist of Items to be Presented at the Sign-off Review

Business Appraisal

- Product cost based upon actual production with targets calculated for increased volumes and savings due to the learner curve experience. The life-cycle for the product and the market should also be presented with a statement of the overall market stability.
- Sales forecast confirming the present order book and the confidence level for projected sales.
- Marketing plan for existing and potential customers matched to the market trends and customers' needs. The plan should also examine competitors' activities and competitive benchmark performances that may attract existing customers.
- Commercial review of actual performance against project planned expenditure and the final business case using the actual non-recurring costs, known product costs and any recurring project expenditure.

Technical Appraisal

- Customer, including

  - production problems resolved; and
  - delivery schedules and volumes confirmed.

- Design changes implemented and design sealed.
- Manufacturing quality, including:

  - quality procedures fully-implemented and people trained;
  - supplier problems still outstanding;
  - customer inspection reports for quality and delivery performance;
  - engineering analysis on any returned units with cause for rejection;
  - audits on the processes complete and accepted by the customer;
  - external audits from independent inspectors/approval authorities completed.

- Production capability including:

  - production volumes delivered against customers' schedules;
  - process capability values for critical features;
  - production capacity and ways to increase production;
  - availability of skilled workforce and status of training programme;
  - confirmation that the product meets the customers' requirements; and
  - cost-reduction and continuous improvement programmes.

- Production confidence including:

  - reject rates and the cost of quality documented with improvement targets;
  - lead-times through the factory known with plans for reduction;
  - cycle-times on the bottleneck processes used to determine target lead-times;
  - statement made on the capability of manufacturing, assembly, test and inspection processes;
  - tool life, tooling and consumable costs calculated with savings agreed;

- o changeover times on key machines included in continuous improvement plans;
- o machine reliability and availability monitored; and
- o shift patterns and payment schemes discussed with the work-force.

- Documentation, including:

  - o quality manuals translated into shop-floor working practices;
  - o shop floor documentation and control systems implemented; and
  - o service manuals published.

- Health safety and the environment, including:

  - o risks and hazards identified;
  - o control procedures implemented; and
  - o environmental impact of the product and processes noted.

Programme and Project Management

- Project-file closure report finalised and handed over to operations.
- Lessons learnt documented and relevant training material developed.
- Project-planning information reviewed and archived.

This marks the end of the project and should be formally acknowledged through the release of a project summary report, and the team disbanded with people assigned to other work.

PROJECT MANAGEMENT

This is an essential element of the product introduction process relying upon the integration of project management to create a product introduction management process. The project manager is responsible for managing the overall project and providing the mechanism for coordinating activities. Consequently, a management process has to be developed that meets the requirements of the business and uses the concepts of good project management practice.

A project manager responsible for managing the introduction of a new product has a demanding task in building the team and carrying responsibility for meeting the project deliverables. It is important that the role of the programme manager is fully understood, giving them authority to take the necessary decisions within the agreed plan parameters and being accountable for owning the expenditure budget, purchasing resources from appropriate managers. The project management role specific to the introduction of a new product:

- Owns the project and delivers the project objectives, rigorously applying the product introduction process and using a defined programme and project management procedure.
- Coordinates the agreements for the product specification and contractual terms with customers.
- Leads the negotiation with customers to recover any additional expenditure for work not covered in the agreed contract/customer order.
- Agrees the technical performance of the product with the chief engineer against contractual commitments.
- Provides an interface to the customer and takes responsibility for ensuring any payments are made, order amendments accepted and the quality of work meets customers' expectations.
- Reports to the customer in a manner required by the customer.
- In conjunction with marketing and engineering, prepares the business case for the approvals required throughout the opportunity evaluation phase.
- Takes responsibility for ensuring that detailed commercial contract negotiations are finalised, and understands the commitments being made on behalf of the company.
- Secures wherever possible customer funds and external grants to recover project expenditure.
- Ensures patents are established in appropriate territories to protect proprietary knowledge whenever possible.
- Reviews and controls the release of confidential information presented in the technical press, conferences and other publications.

These and other project management activities for large projects may require work packages to be assigned to different people, creating a management structure where project managers responsible for various parts report to a programme manager who coordinates the overall project.

SUMMARY

The elements presented in this section are the crucial aspects of a new product introduction process that the business must manage to ensure that products are developed on time to meet the market requirements. It is essential to establish the level of financial commitments that are being made to customers, ensuring that finite technical resources are directed towards those projects that have the greatest potential for providing on-going production and the creation of satisfactory returns for all stakeholders in the company.

5

Supply-chain Management

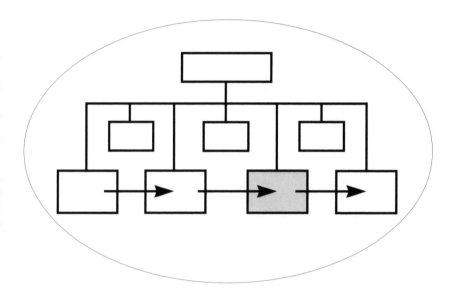

Topics

Overview
Strategic sourcing
Factory space and location
Manufacturing systems and equipment
Assembly and test activities
Machining facilities
Internal factory capacity
Production planning and control
Measures of performance
Organisation
Quality systems
Human resources
New product introduction process
Summary

5

Supply-chain Management

OVERVIEW

Fundamental to achieving demanding business performance objectives is having an effective supply-chain, designed to be competitive in international markets. To be commercially successful, a strong customer and product base has to be developed and continually enhanced, which results in the need for an inherently flexible manufacturing system that can be readily adapted to satisfy customers' requirements. Good businesses have well-developed formal and informal two-way communication systems, and everybody in the organisation fully understands the goals and challenges facing the business. This is supported by senior management making time to 'walk the factory', and obtain comments directly from the workforce.

Although manufacturing operations differ, it is important that companies have a consistent approach for determining how the supply-chain should be designed to meet the demands of particular market sectors. An attempt will be made to describe the key requirements of a supply-chain process and identify the elements of good supply-chain practice. The check-lists at the end of each section have been devised using my experience of supply-chain operations. It is not possible to compile a generic list because of the diversity of manufacturing operations, but many of the items should be relevant to most machine-based manufacturing facilities. Identifying areas for improvement is not generally the major problem; the important task is to establish which items are the most critical to the business and will lead to significant improvements in performance. This can only be achieved through intimate knowledge of the supply-chain, but all businesses need a foundation of:

- Production planning – knowing what has to be made.
- Sourcing and material control – having materials available for manufacture.

139

- Good machine capability – manufacturing parts to drawing
- Continual improvement – eliminating all types of waste.

The check lists can be used to confirm items that are relevant to a particular supply chain, and then under *status* establish whether the item has been:

Fin   Item *finished* and fully operational.
Imp   Item in the process of being *implemented.*
Pln   Item *planned* ready for implementation.

Experience has demonstrated that good supply-chain processes are developed over considerably long periods, requiring consistent attention to detail aimed at removing variability and unplanned events from the process. These lists appear relatively long, but in many instances items can be implemented with little or no expenditure; only management commitment is needed to define and monitor the regular tasks people have to perform, and a belief that teamwork is more effective than individual effort.

STRATEGIC SOURCING

All businesses should conduct a strategic 'Make vs Buy' analysis to identify those items that encapsulate the business' proprietary knowledge, or enhance the customers' perceived value of the technical contribution. This task is strategically important for the business because it:

- Determines future investments in both product and process development;
- Makes the business dependent upon key suppliers for non-strategic components;
- Creates excess capacity within the factory, resulting from more purchased items;
- Changes the skills requirement towards purchasing, logistics and quality assessment;
- Provides a mechanism for reducing the cost base of the business; and
- Reduces the level of vertical integration.

If out-sourcing is used to provide a short-term cost reduction opportunity, it may result in the out-placement of critical items with dire long-term consequences, for example having to purchase critical components from a major competitor.

Internal supply-chain activities should focus upon producing core components, assembly, test, and aftermarket support. Manufacturing facilities should be modular, designed to satisfy the customer's requirements and maintain a consistent flow of work through the cells. Care should be taken to analyse the supply chain in terms of *runner, repeater, stranger* products (p. 41) to ensure the manufacturing system is compatible with the type of products being made.

Purchased components and sub-assemblies should be bought out as complete items with the supplier taking responsibility for any additional processing necessary to complete the job. Components to be made in house should also have first-stage operations performed by the material supplier, to minimise the total acquisition costs and the time materials are retained on site. Materials and components should be procured from a small number of selected, quality-approved suppliers who are willing to act in partnership, sharing a proportion of the product introduction risk, introducing innovation that ensures being competitive on total acquisition costs, and matching deliveries to meet changing customers' schedules. Suppliers must also provide long-term supply assurances that protect availability throughout the product life-cycle, and take full responsibility for supplying a quality-assured product on time directly to the assembly area.

These activities are generally the responsibility of a supplies module team that manages the supplier development activities, and ensures quality-assured materials are available to meet the master production schedules.

FACTORY SPACE AND LOCATION

Companies must retain a minimum number of factories needed to meet the business objectives and maintain an adequate return on investment. Many businesses have acquired excess factory space, duplicating internal resources for similar components. This has been exacerbated by out-sourcing, and the introduction of high-technology equipment that needs running on extended hours to justify the

Strategic sourcing check-list

Ref	Operational practices	Relevant		Status		
		Yes	No	Fin	Imp	Pln
1	Methodology agreed for taking make vs buy decisions					
2	Make vs buy key aspect of product introduction process					
3	Worldwide sources reviewed for high expenditure items					
4	Vertical integration in-line with industry sector norm					
5	Core competencies for the business defined and agreed					
6	Supplies module responsible for supplier performance					
7	Budget for developing sourcing process established					
8	Resources needed for new product introduction available					
9	Cost model developed to provide accurate comparisons					
10	Supplier rationalisation programme established					
11	Strategic sources identified for non-core components					
12	Supplier-development resource available to key suppliers					
13	Resources allocated to supplier quality assurance					
14	Long-term contracts negotiated, providing cost savings					
15	Parts classified on bills of material for purchased items					
16	Training material developed to increase skill bases					
17	Personal development plans to expand skills agreed					
18	Suppliers' quality measures give meaningful information					
19	Suppliers' delivery performance supports production plan					
20	Suppliers' quality approved to deliver direct to assembly					
21	Internal manufacturing cells redesigned after make vs buy					

Strategic sourcing check-list continued

Ref	Operational practices	Relevant		Status		
		Yes	No	Fin	Imp	Pln
22	Components analysed into runners, repeaters, strangers					
23	Supply-chain interfaces provide consistent work-flow					
24	Parts arrive from suppliers ready for use in the factory					
25	Parts protected from physical and environmental damage					
26	Paperwork rationalised to remove unnecessary tasks					
27	Electronic links established for paperless transactions					
28	Methods for agreeing production schedules established					
29	Rules agreed for setting and changing delivery schedules					
30	Suppliers support continuous improvement programmes					
31	Suppliers involved in product introduction and innovation					
32	Suppliers willing to act in partnership and share risks					
33	Suppliers able to provide long-term supply assurances					
34	Process capability of suppliers' equipment known					
35	Suppliers provide assignment stock when appropriate					
36	Key suppliers have capability for making daily shipments					
37	Strategic suppliers establish customer-focused module					
38	Low-value standard items, 2-bin automatic reordering					
39	Internal facilities considered for sourcing components					
40	Self-billing used with major suppliers					
41	Blanket orders with preferred suppliers for running items					
42	Suppliers paid on time as agreed in the contract					

Factory space and location check-list

Ref	Operational practices	Relevant		Status		
		Yes	No	Fin	Imp	Pln
Footprint of factories established:						
1	Location – state – country – region					
2	Owner of facility					
3	Area of site					
4	Area of offices, production, workshops, warehouses					
5	Space in current use					
Number of people employed on site in:						
6	Sales, product introduction, supply chain, distribution					
7	Main activities conducted on site					
8	Summary of product base					
9	Core processes that must be retained in-house					
10	Major customers					
11	Justification for maintaining site					
12	Cost index of site					
13	Cost index of workforce					
14	Quality performance					
15	Significant investments made in facilities					
16	Shift patterns					
17	Opportunities for increasing output					
18	Links with other business in the company					
19	Opportunities for consolidation					
20	Key items of capital equipment					
21	Average age of plant and equipment					
22	Age of buildings					
23	Matrix of facilities information-evaluated					
24	Site rationalisation plan developed					
25	Consolidation of core component manufacture reviewed					
26	Worldwide locations considered for new facilities					
27	Overall site strategy agreed					
28	Property database established					
29	Impact on profit and cash of relocating sites calculated					
30	Reaction of the customer-base discussed					
31	Method of site disposal identified					
32	Costs of environmental clean-up fully understood					

investment. These new machines generally require less space than those being replaced. All site relocation and consolidation is traumatic; and a thorough evaluation must be undertaken to ensure core skills are retained within the business. This means processes need to be fully capable and documented, with people adequately trained prior to moving.

Understanding the capacity across factories is critical to determining the cost base of the business. The removal of fixed overheads through the consolidation of operations has been an obvious method for large companies to improve overall short-term profitability, but uncertainties in the transition period can result in a significant loss of business, unless managed very professionally.

MANUFACTURING SYSTEM AND EQUIPMENT

These differ with the type of processes performed within the factory, but the following attributes should be clearly visible:

- The layout and appearance of facilities should provide a competitive edge to winning new business from existing and potential customers.
- Minimum factory space should be devoted to offices, with support functions integrated into factory activities.
- The manufacturing system should be rigorously designed, operated on minimum lead-times throughout the supply chain, and be committed to achieving customers' delivery dates.
- People should work in teams with cells structured around natural business processes.
- Team leaders should take responsibility for identifying problems and champion continual improvement.
- Teams and facilities should be designated to make a product or family of components, and flexibly structured to manufacture economically with minimal changeover times.
- Cells should be identified by clear boundaries, appropriate colour schemes and treated floors.
- The business systems should be integral with the manufacturing processes, enabling a rapid response to changes in market demand and customers' schedules.

- Key performance measures for the business and the cell should be maintained, displayed and understood by all members of the team.
- Process and equipment technological know-how should be developed internally to protect proprietary knowledge and safeguard competitive advantage.
- All processes must have a known level of process capability, based upon statistical methods to verify the capability of key operations for critical characteristics, and backed by effective training of team members to use quality techniques.
- The team must take full responsibility for the quality of their work, with the goal of achieving zero-defect production without any indirect inspection or rework.
- The factory must provide a safe working environment with full account being taken of existing and new processes on health safety and the natural environment.
- All cells should strive to implement best practice in:

  o cross-training of staff;
  o continual development and application of standard working practices;
  o on-line quality systems;
  o daily stand-up meetings;
  o progressive reduction of changeover times;
  o continual attack on lead-times;
  o commitment to reducing batch sizes, matching customer call-off quantities;
  o total involvement in continuous improvement;
  o implementation of productive maintenance;
  o customer orientated measures of performance; and
  o visible self-audit system for demonstrating conformance to procedures.

- Bottleneck processes must be identified and kept running as a priority to other jobs.
- Key machines and test rigs must be identified and utilisation monitored.
- Where possible, productivity should be maximised, investment minimised, and continuous improvement promoted by using appropriate material transfer systems between cells, stop-on-fault mechanisms, error-prevention devices, and ergonomic workplaces.

Manufacturing systems and equipment check-list

Ref	Operational practices	Relevant		Status		
		Yes	No	Fin	Imp	Pln
1	Manufacturing facilities appropriate to the task					
2	Appearance of facilities provides customer confidence					
3	Layout of factory orientated to customers' requirements					
4	Minimum factory space devoted to production offices					
5	Support functions integrated into factory activities					
6	Supply chains designed to meet the business needs					
7	Manufacturing systems developed for minimum lead-time					
8	Bottleneck process must be identified and not interrupted					
9	Everybody committed to achieving known delivery dates					
10	People work in small teams with identified team leader					
11	Team leader organises work, and identifies problems					
12	Regular group meetings to resolve day-to-day problems					
13	Continual improvement groups supported with resources					
14	Teams structured to produce a defined set of parts					
15	Team takes responsibility for quality of own work					
16	People multiskilled to perform variety of tasks in team					
17	Goal of zero defects with no indirect inspection accepted					
18	Teams flexibly structured to produce economically					
19	Cells identified with clear boundaries					
20	Factory floor coated, kept clean and well-maintained					
21	Working areas kept clean by team					

Manufacturing system and equipment check-list continued

Ref	Operational practices	Relevant		Status		
		Yes	No	Fin	Imp	Pln
22	Team responsible for routine checks on equipment					
23	Management and team audits made on state of plant					
24	Tooling and fixtures cleaned and stored appropriately					
25	Preventive maintenance built into loading schedules					
26	Equipment cleaned, bolts tightened, minor faults rectified					
27	Planned: coolant, filter and slurry tank maintenance					
28	Metal particle skimmers on grinding machine coolants					
29	Guarding on equipment in good working order					
30	Noise eliminated or controlled with acoustic protectors					
31	Fluid leaks on equipment rectified immediately					
32	Space around equipment clean and free from oil seepage					
33	Process knowledge documented and regularly updated					
34	Proprietary manufacturing processes guarded and valued					
35	Lead times continually challenged and reduced					
36	Change-over of processes planned, techniques developed					
37	Stocks/work in progress are *not* regarded as an asset					
38	Batch sizes established based upon *Takt* times					
39	All processes have known level of process capability					
40	Factory provides a safe working environment					
41	Processes are operated in a accordance with legislation					
42	Standard working practices documented and followed					
43	On the job training provided by team members					

ASSEMBLY AND TEST ACTIVITIES

Assembly and test are usually regarded as the core processes that must be retained in-house and integrated into modules that:

- handle a range of products within the product family;
- have ready access to assembly equipment and test facilities with sufficient flexibility for handling all designated products;
- embrace activities driven by the master production schedule, accurately translating the customer's delivery requirements, and ensuring components are available prior to starting assembly;
- include team of multiskilled workers capable of performing all activities and responsible for assembling and testing products, including final conformance, rectification, verification and packing of products ready for dispatch; and
- pack products ready for use by the customer, in containers identifying the supplier, and protecting contents from physical and environmental damage.

MACHINING FACILITIES

These should be organised into modules, designed to produce a range of critical components associated with a family of parts in a way that does not compromise the efficient manufacture of high volume items:

- Machining cells should undertake all the processes needed to complete components, including deburring, part-marking, studding, and building sub-assemblies, taking full responsibility for supplying quality-assured parts direct to the assembly module.
- Machining operations should be eliminated, with investment in standard modern equipment capable of performing multiple operations in one set-up whenever it can be commercially justified.
- Production lead-times should be reduced by minimising the number of machining operations required to complete components, and systematically reducing the time components are waiting for operations.
- A team of people organised by a working team leader should take full responsibility for operating a group of machines, providing first-line maintenance, verifying process capability, and performing necessary in-cycle operations.

Assembly and test activities check-list

Ref	Operational practices	Relevant		Status		
		Yes	No	Fin	Imp	Pln
1	Assembly system designed to handle a range of products					
2	Assembly and test equipment suitable for product range					
3	Equipment flexible and able to perform necessary tests					
4	Activities driven by master production schedule					
5	All parts available prior to starting assembly operation					
6	Parts routinely cleaned and examined prior to assembly					
7	Products assembled and tested by multiskilled team					
8	Team performs any rectification and final conformance					
9	Products packed ready for use by the customer					
10	Containers protect the product from physical damage					
11	Packaging provides adequate environmental protection					
12	Products clearly marked, identifying the company					
13	Assembly tools and fixtures dedicated to product family					

- Material movement must be synchronised to achieve a continuous flow of work, minimising work-in-progress and lead-times.
- Materials should be held in their lowest cost state consistent with meeting customer service requirements.

INTERNAL FACTORY CAPACITY

Determining and controlling manufacturing capacity is one of management's most difficult tasks. Adjusting capacity to meet fluctua-

Assembly and test activities check-list continued

Ref	Operational practices	Relevant		Status		
		Yes	No	Fin	Imp	Pln
14	Test equipment specified in control documentation					
15	Appropriate containers available for kits of parts					
16	Assembly area conforms to appropriate cleanliness level					
17	Practices documented emphasising critical characteristics					
18	Equipment calibrated against known standards					
19	Verification system and calibration records maintained					
20	Routine maintenance built into test schedules					
21	Correlation checks made on similar test stands					
22	Test rig services: air, fluids, etc checked to specification					
23	Power tools to aid assembly operation installed					
24	Assembly station ergonomically designed					
25	Lighting levels above factory statutory requirements					
26	Repetitive tasks automated to prevent operator strain					

tions in demand is generally achieved through changing work patterns or the number of people employed. This method works well for seasonal and minor changes in demand, but has limits that then require a redesign of the supply-chain and manufacturing facilities.

Facilities requiring a significant investment in capital equipment must plan to operate on a minimum of two full shifts, allowing the third shift for changes in output and providing time for routine maintenance and process development. However, modern high-capital-intensive plants should plan to run 24 hours per day, using lower premium continental shift patterns for operating seven days a week.

Machining facilities check-list

Ref	Operational practices	Relevant		Status		
		Yes	No	Fin	Imp	Pln
1	Machining modules established for families of parts					
2	Cells perform all tasks needed to complete components					
3	Responsibility taken for providing quality-assured parts					
4	Deliver components directly to the assembly module					
5	Systematic approach for removing machining operations					
6	Continual cost evaluation for exploiting new technology					
7	Lead-times of components awaiting machining reduced					
8	Machine running speeds ensure consistent production					
9	Team of people responsible for a group of machines					
10	*Nagare* principles evaluated for the machining systems					
11	Modules designed to maintain even flow of work					
12	Different manufacturing system for runners and strangers					
13	Bottleneck machine given priority for work/ maintenance					
14	Team responsible for daily checks, first line maintenance					
15	Machine tools routinely monitored for process capability					
16	Measuring systems evaluated for process capability					

Machining facilities check-list continued

Ref	Operational practices	Relevant		Status		
		Yes	No	Fin	Imp	Pln
17	Measuring equipment calibrated on routine basis					
18	Records rigorously maintained on status of equipment					
19	Preventive maintenance applied to all key machines					
20	Key machines checked annually against specification					
21	New plant purchased to specified process capability level					
22	Jigs and fixtures checked, and cleaned, prior to storing					
23	Dedicated tools controlled, pre-set and allocated to parts					
24	Programme established to reduce variety of tools used					
25	Procedure for managing/controlling tools documented					
26	Components are cleaned after machining operations					
27	Containers used for moving parts cleaned as routine					
28	Containers able to be stacked without damaging contents					
29	Parts located separately preventing physical contact					
30	Material movement synchronised for even work-flow					
31	Materials in the cells held to an absolute minimum					
32	Parts held in lowest cost state, consistent with service					

Machining facilities check-list continued

Ref	Operational practices	Relevant		Status		
		Yes	No	Fin	Imp	Pln
33	Manual methods of material transfer used where feasible					
34	Mechanisation stops process on detection of a fault					
35	Error prevention devices integral with process					
36	Temperature and humidity controlled to specified limits					
37	Levels of contamination in cleaning tanks controlled					
38	Flaw detection and inspection have appropriate lighting					
39	Overall lighting levels better than statutory requirements					
	Plating and heat-treatment					
40	Regular checks and monitors on all plating solutions					
41	Condition of tanks routinely checked and kept clean					
42	Waste products handled and disposed of in safe manner					
43	Plating thickness checked over the complete surface					
44	Processes verified using control chart, confirm capability					
45	Systematic checks on furnace temperature distribution					
46	Thermocouples and heating elements working/ calibrated					
47	Test pieces compatible with part being treated					
48	Area clean with good extraction and ventilation					

Adopting these working arrangements, linked to the out-sourcing of non-core components usually results in a need for less space, and the possible closure of less productive factories. The continual economic pressure for reducing product costs, achieved through consolidating facilities, means that overseas locations with lower labour costs must also be considered when siting new factories and facilities.

Contracts of employment must also be structured, allowing the business to adjust manpower levels to meet the variations in customer demand economically, sometimes at short notice.

Internal factory capacity check-list

Ref	Operational practices	Relevant		Status		
		Yes	No	Fin	Imp	Pln
1	Mechanism exists for determining capacity of the plant					
2	Constraints on output understood, bottlenecks identified					
3	Method of measuring output and effectiveness reliable					
4	Cell capacity calculated and agreed with cell team					
5	Overall plant capacity verified by summation of cell loads					
6	Bottleneck processes used to set pace of production					
7	Key machines run three shifts before installing capacity					
8	Areas work two full shifts before expanding facilities					
9	Maintenance schedules included in overall capacity plan					
10	Methods agreed for adapting capacity to customer needs					
11	Alternative shift patterns considered and reviewed					
12	Total capacity across all sites examined for consolidation					
13	Contracts of employment provide workforce flexibility					

PRODUCTION PLANNING AND CONTROL

All supply chains need to work to an agreed *master production schedule*. This should be owned by the business general manager and established by a cross-functional scheduling committee that coordinates the customer requirements, production capacity, materials availability and the product introduction development requirements across the business. This master production schedule must accurately translate the customer commitments, and be underpinned by capacity plans, detailed cell schedules and confirmed supplier delivery dates.

Constructing the master schedule (particularly for items required on short lead-times) is a complex task and may require an accurate sales forecast to ensure materials and components are available to meet commercially accepted delivery lead-times. Manufacturing operations must work on a *just-in-time* basis with suppliers and customers, ensuring that inventory levels are kept to a minimum whilst protecting customer deliveries.

- The requirement is to respond rapidly to changes in customer demand and have short factory lead-times that make products available to the customer before materials and components are paid for, thus using minimum working capital.
- The material control system should be based upon simple visual systems, requiring reduced levels of central computer support. Bills of material, material requirements planning and sales order processing need integrating on a common database. However, commercially available computerised production scheduling systems are too difficult to maintain, due to the sheer volume of data, if expected to handle all the low-value items listed on the bill of materials.
- Items should be classified, identifying how they should be treated on the material acquisition plan. Generally, 80 per cent of inventory costs are associated with 20 per cent of the part numbers. Low-cost standard items should be handled using a 2-bin automatic re-ordering system to remove complexity from the system.

MEASURES OF PERFORMANCE

The performance of the key processes should be displayed and team members given responsibility for collecting the information. This

Production planning and control check-list

Ref	Operational practices	Relevant		Status		
		Yes	No	Fin	Imp	Pln
1	Master production schedule owned by general manager					
2	Master production schedule identifies long-term capacity					
3	Production schedule establishes materials requirements					
4	Production plan gives commitment for reporting period					
5	Schedules cover *all* the demands placed on production					
6	Production plan verified against known factory capacity					
7	Team leaders agree and commit to delivering plan					
8	System used for coordinating people, machines, materials					
9	Material categorised by usage, value, source, application					
10	Alternative scheduling methods used for different cells					
11	MRP simplified by removing low-value items					
12	Special small items kitted by vendor ready for use					
13	Accuracy on the computer database greater than 98%					
14	Computer up-time greater than 99%					
15	*Kanban* used to pull work through cells, when applicable					
16	Factory works *just-in-time* pulling work into assembly					
17	Material flow between cells controlled by simple systems					
18	Once in process, part is completed with minimum queues					
19	Team determines own work-to list to meet commitment					

should be relevant and comprise financial and non-financial information. Time must be allowed for the team leader or appropriate manager to collectively discuss the findings and identify any corrective actions that are needed to improve the overall performance level. Local measures of performance should focus upon:

- Customer satisfaction;
- Achievement of committed delivery dates;
- Achievement of the production schedules, lead times, reducing

Measures of performance check-list

Ref	Operational practices	Relevant		Status		
		Yes	No	Fin	Imp	Pln
Customer measures						
1	Customer performance – quality, price, and delivery					
2	Cost of quality as % of sales					
3	Cost of quality assurance activity					
4	Cost of internal failure, rework, scrap, rectification					
5	Cost of external failure, returns, recalls, modifications					
6	Product conformance, number of concessions accepted					
7	Equipment returns/dispatches					
Labour capacity						
8	Hours worked in period					
9	Number of units produced/hour worked					
10	Number of people employed, employees, sub-contractors					
11	Sales per employee					
12	Added value per unit of pay					
13	Overtime worked					
14	Training hours per employee					
15	Unplanned down-time					
16	Industrial accidents					
17	Environmental incidents					
18	% cost bought out/sales					
19	% cost direct labour/sales					

work in progress, improving quality, and overall capability of the processes;
- Cost reductions and achievement of target production costs; and
- Continuous improvement plans and achievements.

Information must be presented in an understandable form, preferably using suitable graphs to illustrate trends, with upward movement showing improvement.

Measures of performance check-list continued

Ref	Operational practices	Relevant		Status		
		Yes	No	Fin	Imp	Pln
20	% cost factory support/sales					
21	% cost overheads/sales					
22	Number of key machine tools					
23	% Utilisation of key machine tools					
24	% of processes known to be process capable					
	Schedule adherence					
25	Value of planned MPS/sales					
26	% achievement of the MPS					
27	% achievement of OE deliveries to customer requirement					
28	% achievement of spares sent by customer request date					
29	Service-level deliveries made to agreed turn round time					
30	Supplier delivery performance to purchase schedule					
31	Average lead-time for in-house manufacture					
32	Average lead-time for bought-out items/materials					
	Stocks					
33	Stock turns					
34	% stock held as raw materials					
35	% stock held as bought out components					
36	% work in progress					
37	% finished goods					

ORGANISATION

Supply-chain processes should operate with a maximum of four levels, from general manager to shop-floor, with overheads subject to constant review for possible cost savings. The leadership style will encourage:

- Open two-way communication;
- Team responsibility for all activities;
- Continuous improvement through teamwork and cell-based initiatives;
- Commitment to creating a clean effective working environment;
- Project management disciplines to drive change programmes; and
- Payment systems recognising skill levels and team contributions.

Full-time project managers should be assigned to significant change programmes, supported by full and part-time task forces dedicated to

Organisation check-list

Ref	Operational practices	Relevant		Status		
		Yes	No	Fin	Imp	Pln
1	Supply-chain operates with maximum of four levels					
2	Overheads justified by determining how they add value					
3	Business organised around core processes					
4	One person owns the supply-chain process					
5	Core processes designed to meet business requirements					
6	Teams established responsible for a product or process					
7	Teams responsible for all activities, led by team leader					
8	Continuous improvement integrated into normal working					
9	Commitment to provide clean, safe, effective workplace					

delivering the operational improvements and strategic challenges identified in the business plan.

QUALITY SYSTEMS

All businesses should develop a quality system conforming to ISO 9000. It must be designed and implemented to require minimum bureaucracy, and certified by an accredited third party. Procedures, once established, should be documented in collaboration with the cell teams and followed rigorously, until up-dated by incorporating recommendations identified by continuous improvement groups.

All customer problems must trigger structured corrective actions, based upon applying teamwork to identify the root cause, resolving the problem, and preventing its re-occurrence. The quality system must also incorporate a manufacturing change control procedure that integrates with the engineering change control system.

Organisation check-list continued

Ref	Operational practices	Relevant		Status		
		Yes	No	Fin	Imp	Pln
10	Project management disciplines used to support change					
11	Structure for training manufacturing engineers created					
12	Reward structure for professional engineers established					
13	Engineers involved in customer development process					
14	Engineers seconded to product introduction teams					
15	Cell team members consulted on product introduction					
16	Resources and time allocated for improvement projects					
17	Time identified and allowed for training					
18	Payment system recognises skill levels and contribution					

Quality systems check-list

Ref	Operational practices	Relevant		Status		
		Yes	No	Fin	Imp	Pln
1	Business quality system conforms to ISO 9000					
2	Quality system written for a minimum of bureaucracy					
3	Verified against actual working practice					
4	People trained and tested in the procedures					
5	Accredited by approved third party					
6	Customer problem triggers root-cause analysis of events					
7	Team approach used to implement corrective actions					
8	Record maintained of changes to process and procedures					
9	Key characteristics identified for controlled processes					
10	Documentation understandable and appropriate					
11	Methods verify compliance for critical characteristics					
12	Documentation checked for conforming to latest release					
13	Process planning sheets give graphical work instructions					

HUMAN RESOURCES

All employees should be:

- Able to share a common employment environment, including working conditions and arrangements.
- Able to participate in a continuous personal development programme, linked to an effective system of personal performance appraisal and monitoring of training needs, leading to proficiency in a range of skills allowing flexibility and job rotation.

Quality systems check-list continued

Ref	Operational practices	Relevant		Status		
		Yes	No	Fin	Imp	Pln
14	Quality records on separate sheet to process instructions					
15	First article inspection report verified to work instruction					
16	Assembly processes supported by graphical information					
17	System-generated records subject to document control					
18	Records maintained on calibration of measuring systems					
19	Re-calibration rigorously performed at specified intervals					
20	Machine-tool capability verified using statistical methods					
21	Measuring systems checked for suitability of process					
22	Measuring equipment owned by the company					
23	Measuring equipment clean, protected when not in use					
24	Product conformance verified using customer techniques					
25	Routine management quality audits conducted					

- Committed to providing customer satisfaction and continual process improvements.
- Able to work in a team, and contribute to enhancing team performance through involvement in continuous improvement groups.
- Proud of their work, taking full responsibility for product quality and verification of conformance to specification.
- Dedicated to enhancing quality, whilst continually reducing costs.
- Willing to work flexible hours (when required) to meet variations in work-load.
- Rewarded in a fair and equitable manner.

Human resources check-list

Ref	Operational practices	Relevant		Status		
		Yes	No	Fin	Imp	Pln
1	Formal and informal communication system established					
2	Business goals disseminated, understood by workforce					
3	Challenges facing the business communicated openly					
4	Management listen to feedback from workforce					
5	Formal employee survey conducted to gauge perceptions					
6	Senior managers make time to walk round factory					
7	Managers discuss issues first-hand with the workforce					
8	Same conditions of employment and work arrangements					
9	Everyone able to participate in personal development					
10	Performance appraisals used to monitor training needs					
11	People encouraged to be proficient at a range of skills					
12	Job-rotation and flexible working as accepted practices					
13	Importance of customer satisfaction fully understood					
14	Total commitment to team work and supporting the group					
15	Continuous improvement and enhancement of working practices					
16	Everybody able to stop a process compromising quality					
17	Dedicated to delivering quality whilst reducing costs					
18	Reward systems equitable, providing fair return for effort					
19	Regular group meetings to inform and resolve problems					

Human resources check-list continued

Ref	Operational practices	Relevant		Status		
		Yes	No	Fin	Imp	Pln
20	Several people trained in problem-solving techniques:					
21	Pareto analysis					
22	brainstorming					
23	cause-and-effect diagrams					
24	drawing graphs and isoplots					
25	process flow charts					
26	process-charting with respect to quantity or time					
27	making process capability calculations					
28	first-line maintenance requirements					
29	Records of people's skill range and level of proficiency					
30	Safety glasses worn in designated areas					
31	Hearing checks routine and documented					
32	Eyesight checked on routine basis					
33	Eating and drinking confined to designated areas					
34	People given on-the-job training, tested for proficiency					
35	People trained prior to being asked to perform the task					
36	Alcohol or drug abuse acknowledged and help offered					
37	Ethics programme instigated to ensure contract compliance					
38	Health, safety and environment procedures documented					
39	Any HS&E issue given priority and immediate resolution					
40	Formal group reviews and actions on HS&E matters					
41	Clean overalls made available giving pride of association					

NEW PRODUCT INTRODUCTION PROCESS

All businesses should integrate manufacturing engineers into the product introduction teams, ensuring new components are designed whenever possible to fit within the capacity envelopes of existing manufacturing equipment and tooling. Disciplines must be applied for controlling a variety of components, tooling, fixtures and assemblies, taking into account the size of tooling carousels and the impact of changeovers on production output.

New product programmes should exploit existing competencies; new ones should only be developed in technologies identified as strategic, by the make vs buy analysis conducted as part of the product introduction process.

SUMMARY

Efficient supply-chain systems can be achieved through a process of continual improvement. However, the most effective ones are the result of a good manufacturing system design that is refined through involving the workforce to implement continuous improvements. The manufacturing system for new products should be designed as an integral part of the product introduction process, but this generally leaves other manufacturing areas used for existing products with suboptimum processes. These areas should also be the subject of a separate supply-chain redesign programme aimed at improving effectiveness and reducing costs.

Manufacturing systems design is a specialist activity normally undertaken by a multidisciplinary team directed by a project manager. They collectively analyse and design an appropriate supply-chain system using the following procedures:

- Data collection from existing processes, material flow, information flow, production volumes, market requirements, production methods, machine capabilities, quality performance, manufacturing procedures and so forth.
- Steady-state design of a more effective manufacturing system based upon a strategic make vs buy analysis, cost-justifiable modern manufacturing methods, flexible manufacturing principles, shorter lead-times, and a multiskilled team approach.

New product introduction check-list

Ref	Operational practices	Relevant		Status		
		Yes	No	Fin	Imp	Pln
1	Manufacturing fully involved in product introduction					
2	Products designed for manufacture					
3	Products designed for assembly					
4	Products designed for maintenance					
5	Manufacturing system designed for new products					
6	Existing facilities redesigned to reduce costs					
7	Investment needed to reduce product costs determined					
8	Alternative viable manufacturing methods evaluated					
9	Components designed for available production processes					
10	Suppliers involved in the design process					
11	Standard parts established and used whenever feasible					
12	Standard tooling used whenever possible					
13	Tooling for new designs must not exceed carousel slots					
14	Tool changes in carousels minimal for rapid changeovers					
15	Components designed for minimising machine setup time					
16	Once inside, all operations to complete the part in-house					
17	Bill of materials owned and updated by design authority					
18	Record of engineering change maintained and controlled					
19	Fault recording and corrective action system established					
20	Product introduction design tools applied to process					
21	Process FMEA used to determine robustness of methods					

- Dynamic system design that considers how the system will operate, incorporating features that make the process robust under a wide variety circumstances.
- Information systems specification and design, ensuring all information is appropriate, has an owner and can be obtained as part of the supply-chain process.
- Control systems design and implementation needed for planning supply-chain activities, confirming the manufacturing facility meets its financial targets and delivers high quality products on time to meet customers' schedules.

Manufacturing system engineers are essential for developing and implementing good supply-chain practices. They are responsible for performing several key tasks within the business, notably:

- Designing the manufacturing processes for new products as an integral part of a product introduction process.
- Developing alternative production methods for new and existing components.
- Designing manufacturing systems and installation of facilities needed to meet overall production requirements.
- Production engineering on components, manufacturing layouts, fixtures, tooling, materials handling and so on, essential for maintaining deliveries and reducing costs.
- Establishing the level of investment needed in plant and equipment, quantifying the return and justifying expenditure.
- Estimating product costs as the basis for making significant business commitments.
- Supporting suppliers to achieve necessary quality standards and delivery dates.

The challenge now is to expand the knowledge and experience of manufacturing engineers and product designers making them capable of encapsulating the breadth of skills needed to support all aspects of customer development, product introduction management and supply-chain processes.

6

Industrial Distribution Management

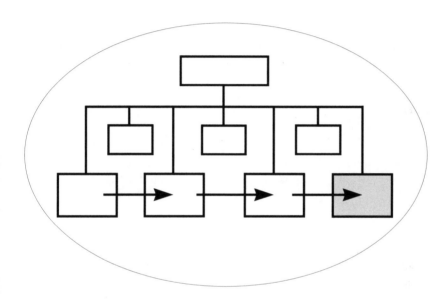

Topics

Introduction
Strategic analysis
Market flowout
Key buying factors by market
  segment
Customer trends and
  forecasting
Strategic local market
  planning
Competitor profile
Market attractiveness

SWOT analysis
Positioning the branch
Tactical sales techniques
Customer selection
Sales planning
Sales action processes
Selling techniques
Sales-force effectiveness
Evaluation and appraisal
Measures of performance
Summary

6

Industrial Distribution Management

INTRODUCTION

Industrial distribution is critical to many businesses because it is the way products are sold across national and international territories. Companies have to develop a number of routes to market, but for commodity-type products having a local presence is a prime factor in securing sales. These distribution outlets can be owned directly by the manufacturing company, or by a third party with expertise in selling a range of products into local markets. In some instances sales are obtained by waiting for customers to identify a supplier, making purchases similar to a local shop. However, for most industrial products, a more structured method for targeting potential customers has to developed if the business is to achieve its commercial goals. In some sectors the distributor also adds value by tailoring the product to meet a specific customer requirement.

This chapter identifies key marketing and planning factors that are the foundation of establishing and managing good industrial distribution businesses. Examples from the fluid power industry in the USA are used to illustrate critical aspects of the process.

STRATEGIC ANALYSIS

Strategic analysis is needed to ensure the management team are fully aware of the external influences that will impact demand for the range of existing products and services, while providing a technique for identifying opportunities for new product lines. Businesses are influenced by several external factors including competition from companies offering similar products, and possible alternative substitute products or services. Therefore a regular review is needed of market segmentation, changes within the industry and the markets served.

The core elements of strategic analysis are associated with the following:

- *Market analysis* including,

  o market flowout showing the product's routes to the customer;
  o key buying factors by market segment or product line;
  o customer trends and forecasting; and
  o strategic local market planning.

- *Economic analysis* including,

  o break-even analysis by product line and business.

- *Competitive analysis* including,

  o competitor profiles;
  o strengths, weaknesses, opportunities and threats (SWOT) analysis; and
  o positioning the branch.

Strategic analysis needs to be undertaken at a national level and repeated if necessary for different world territories. This analysis provides a foundation for the detailed market planning that must be conducted at local level to identify specific opportunities for generating and maintaining sales.

MARKET FLOWOUT

This examines the way products within a family of similar components reach the end customer. Products take several routes from the manufacturer, and it is important to understand the relative importance of these different channels. The example given in Figure 6.1 shows a market flowout for the information shown in Table 6.2 on p. 178.

The figures beside each box give the sales value ($m), and the chart shows the different routes to the end-customers. These may have to be constructed for a number of territories depending upon the market structure. However, the purpose of this chart is to help understand the relative importance of the different channels and ensure that those with the greatest sales potential are not overlooked.

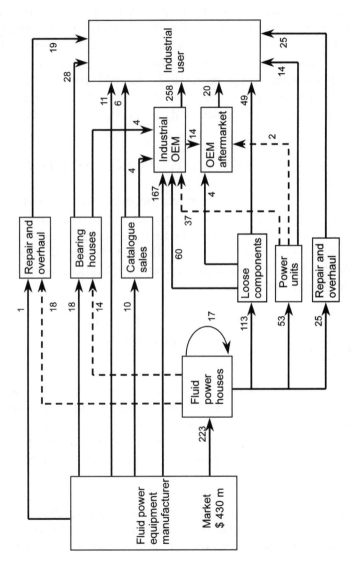

Figure 6.1 Market flowout analysis

Constructing a chart is relatively straightforward using information from, for example, the Department of Industry, trade associations, business performance summary publications, and own company knowledge. Presenting the information in this format gives a clearer perspective on the way products are distributed, and may be instrumental in reformulating the strategic plan, taking greater account of the different routes to reach the end customer. The other factor that should be noted, is that in some instances the distributor also adds value to the products being sold. In the case of the fluid power industry, the distributor often provides a design and manufacturing service for power units and complete systems.

KEY BUYING FACTORS BY MARKET SEGMENT

Customers seeking to purchase a product have a variety of reasons for buying. Products often serve several market sectors and it is important to understand the factors each group uses when making a purchase. These are known as the *key buying factors*. The same product may be sold into different applications and for different purposes, for example:

- New products being introduced into the market;
- Repeat business on existing products; or
- Repair of an existing unit.

The key buying factors will normally be different for each type of application, and these need to be identified and confirmed at a local level to ensure they are relevant. The following example of key buying factors is for fluid power equipment. This industry has a defined market segmentation between industrial and mobile applications, and three different types of customer:

- Original equipment manufacturer (OEM) purchasing systems or components for installation into a range of products;
- User who purchases components needed for repairing or overhauling existing equipment; or
- Re-seller who stocks a range of items that are sold in relatively small numbers, and has to obtain product-lines from a distributor because the account is too small to deal directly with the manufacturer.

Table 6.1 *Key buying factors in order of priority*

	OEM	*User*	*Re-seller*
		Customers served	
Industrial			
New applications	Engineering-driven sales/technical effort brand price delivery/availability	Engineering-driven	
Repeat	Installed-brand driven brand price sales effort delivery/availability inside sales		
Maintenance repair and overhaul		Normal: installed-brand driven installed brand sales effort delivery/availability price	Customer driven installed brand delivery/availability customer service price sales effort
		Emergency: delivery-driven installed brand delivery/availability local presence	
Mobile			
New applications	Engineering-driven brand sales/technical effort price delivery/availability		
Repeat	Installed-brand driven brand price sales effort delivery/availability inside sales		
Maintenance repair and overhaul		Up-time driven delivery/availability sales effort OEM brand customer service price	Delivery-driven sales effort brand delivery/availability local presence customer service price

From the analysis shown in Table 6.1, in these instances, *price* is not regarded as the main reason for securing the sale in any sector. These are almost commodity products in a market that has several established manufacturers offering compatible products. *Brand* was still identified as the key buying factor for customers selecting a particular product, particularly when it was required as a repeat or replacement item.

CUSTOMER TRENDS AND FORECASTING

Understanding market trends and analysing events that will impact future sales is essential for forecasting and planning. It is important to identify:

- Product lines with growth potential;
- Areas that require concentrated selling effort;
- How major competitors will react in the market; and
- Events that will have an impact upon the market.

Government publications are available that plot and discuss industrial trends using the standard industrial classification (SIC) code. Information is also available in trade journals and the technical press.

The **SIC code** is extremely useful, because it is included in many published databases, and can be used as the linking parameter allowing data to be merged, and provide information that is directly relevant to securing sales in particular market sectors.

The example given in Figure 6.2 shows sales for fluid power equipment by major market sector during 1997–98 with projections for the next four years. This provides the overall market trends, enabling judgments to be made concerning the areas of greatest significance. Typical figures for different market segments are shown in Table 6.2.

From these figures mobile and industrial equipment sales are expected to remain static with growth occurring in the application of pneumatics. The market in electro-hydraulics is also expected to increase. Both these groups have benefited from the introduction of new high-technology products with increased functionality, enabling the range of system applications to be expanded.

The next task is to convert this high-level national information, using the market flowout analysis, into a distribution sales forecast. This is achieved by taking the data and factoring the proportion of

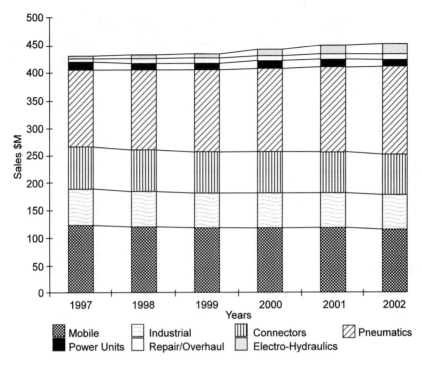

Figure 6.2   Sales by product segment

sales that goes through the distribution channel (see Figure 6.3). These sales are comprised of two elements, those generated through the direct distribution of products, and those value-added sales where the distributor provides additional services.

The added-value content of the fluid power market comprises:

- Fluid power equipment and auxiliary items needed to build a system;
- Work undertaken in specifying the equipment;
- Designing the system and special components needed for a customised solution;
- Manufacturing the non-standard items and assembling the components into a system;
- Commissioning and testing equipment against the design specification; and
- Installing the system and verifying that the overall performance meets the customer's requirements.

Table 6.2 *Sales forecast by major market sectors ($m)*

	1997	1998	1999	2000	2001	2002
Product sales						
Pneumatics	140	144	148	152	154	158
Hydraulics	290	287	288	292	297	297
Total	430	433	436	444	451	455
Sales by product segment						
Mobile	124	122	120	120	121	119
Industrial	66	65	64	64	64	63
Connectors	77	76	75	75	75	74
Pneumatics	140	144	148	152	154	158
Power units	12	12	12	12	12	12
Repair/overhaul	7	8	9	10	9	9
Electro-hydraulics	4	6	8	11	16	20
Total	430	433	436	444	451	455
Distribution product sales						
Mobile	12	13	14	16	18	20
Industrial	22	22	23	24	26	28
Connectors	29	29	29	30	31	31
Pneumatics	49	52	56	64	69	70
Power units	6	6	6	7	7	7
Repair/overhaul	6	7	8	9	8	9
Electro-hydraulics	0	1	1	2	4	6
Total	124	130	137	152	163	171
Value-added content						
Mobile	8	9	10	11	13	14
Industrial	15	15	16	17	18	19
Connectors	29	29	29	30	31	32
Pneumatics	20	21	23	26	28	30
Power units	18	18	19	20	21	22
Repair/overhaul	24	24	23	23	23	23
Electro-hydraulics	2	4	6	9	18	20
Total	116	120	126	136	152	160
Total distribution market	240	250	263	288	315	331

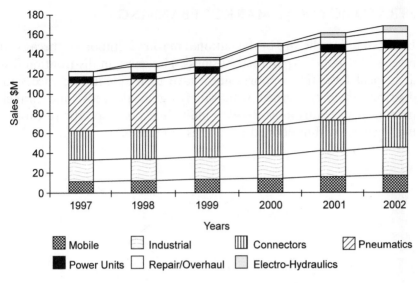

Figure 6.3 Distribution product sales

Figure 6.4 shows typical figures for the volume of sales obtained through selling component, added-value services and building systems.

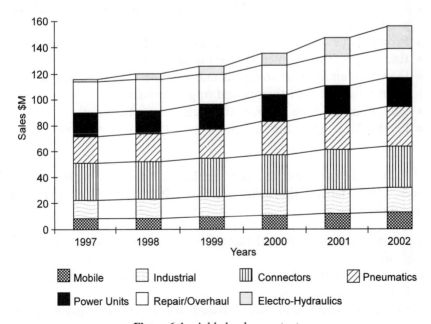

Figure 6.4 Added-value content

STRATEGIC LOCAL MARKET PLANNING

Understanding the size of the national market is important because it reveals the scope of potential business. However, in distribution it is at a local level that opportunities have to be identified; successful distribution is concerned with satisfying local needs, and branch management teams must develop individual plans specific to capturing business within defined territories (Figure 6.5).

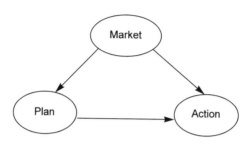

Figure 6.5   Local market planning

At a local level, the market planning process comprises the following elements:

- Estimating the market size by segment and the associated available market-share;
- Profiling the competition and identifying their major customers;
- Ranking market segments in terms of attractiveness;
- Determining internal strengths and weaknesses of the business;
- Identifying external threats and opportunities;
- Determining where to focus the local sales effort; and
- Establishing opportunities and planning actions to obtain more sales.

Estimating the size of the local market and determining the current and future market share has to be evaluated by more than one method:

- Relating computer-based trade directories to an industrial spend-profile.
- Factoring national statistics to a local territory based upon the industrial population.
- Local sales-team assessment based upon the past year's performance.

The first method has considerable potential, exploiting an increasing availability of electronic data and an inherent capability for refinement with subsequent iteration. The technique is based upon estimating (using current experience) the typical customer spend-profile for each category of product, within a particular SIC code classification. These can then be used in conjunction with the local business directory to determine the potential sales volume for each product line within the territory. For example:

SIC	Description	Sales/spend ratio	Segment split (%)						
32452	Kiln manufacturer	2736	0	2	17	9	56	3	13

which means that a kiln manufacturer purchases $1 of fluid power equipment for each $2736 of sales, and is predicted from the business's current experience to spend:

  0% on mobile equipment
  2% on industrial equipment
 17% on connectors
  9% on pneumatics
56% on power units
  3% on repair and overhaul
13% on electro-hydraulics

This distribution profile is then used for similar kiln manufacturers within and outside the territory to determine the overall market potential. The other advantage of using this technique is that it also identifies other kiln manufacturers within the area that are not present customers, leading to possible additional sales.

The local sales team's assessment must always be challenged, because estimates will be constrained by their own narrow perspective of the market, and the natural reluctance to commit to achieving greater sales without personal incentives. And all these estimates must be adjusted for the proportion of products passing through the different routes to market, as identified by the market flowout analysis. This then allows the company's potential sales to be compared against the projected sales within each market segment, and the market-share calculated, thus identifying the opportunity for growth.

COMPETITOR PROFILE

Detailed knowledge of competitors is critical for effective market planning, and considerable effort must be directed to determining the following facts:

- *Who are the major competitors?* This must include similar businesses, and also companies that operate in the other channels identified by the market flowout analysis.
- *What are their strategies?* Which target markets are they focusing upon? What type of value-added services are they offering? How are their businesses structured?
- *How large is the company?* Facts have to be collected on the volume of local and group sales, number of employees and a judgment made on whether they are growing, or in terminal decline.
- *What are their strengths and weaknesses?* These need to be expressed in terms of product lines, services offered, investment in technology (equipment and systems), and skill level of the workforce.
- *What are their reaction patterns?* For example, do they adopt aggressive price-cutting, or are they weak competition?

Marketing is a competitive activity that must be planned in terms of strategy and tactics. Winning the business takes ideas and disciplined thinking and is a battle that must be won.

MARKET ATTRACTIVENESS

Determining which markets have the greatest potential is critical for focusing resources. Many companies waste valuable time, money and effort on seeking business in the wrong market segments. Identifying and understanding the most attractive segments to target resources towards is essential for creating an effective strategy.

There are several ways to rank attractiveness:

- Gross margin;
- Size of potential market;
- Growth rate and new sales opportunities; and
- Nature of competition.

However, the current business climate and market conditions generally dictate that *gross margin* is the prime factor when assessing the attractiveness of a market segment.

(In the fluid power business, maintenance and overhaul has the best gross margin followed by industrial equipment, mobile components, power units and pneumatics.)

STRENGTHS, WEAKNESSES, OPPORTUNITIES AND THREATS (SWOT) ANALYSIS

A SWOT analysis summarises the main issues that are facing the branch or distribution centre when preparing a local business plan. Strengths and weaknesses refer to inside factors affecting the businesses. Opportunities and threats refer to the outside factors that may impact the future of the business. Each item must be presented in a form that identifies possible actions that should be considered to redress particular situations. Success within a local territory depends upon responding to the changes in the market, and these must be closely linked to the strengths and weaknesses of the branch. Action must be taken that exploits strengths and corrects weaknesses.

The development of the type of grid shown in Figure 6.6 is often successfully accomplished by involving the local sales and branch personnel in conjunction with the business management team.

STRENGTHS	WEAKNESSES
Distributes full range of components Brand leader for industrial equipment Large number of industrial customers Franchise covers wide area	Poor range of pneumatic components No systems design capability Hose and fittings supplied by specialist Sales people have limited technical capability
OPPORTUNITIES	THREATS
Develop one stop shop for all services Establish power unit manufacturing facility Purchase good pneumatic range of equipment Develop mobile equipment expertise	Catalogue houses supplying industrial companies directly Lose key franchise to competitor Companies failing to pay bills on time New technology equipment not available

Figure 6.6 SWOT analysis grid for a fluid power distributor

POSITIONING THE BRANCH

The heart of modern strategic marketing is segmentation, targeting and positioning. The objective is to relate the most attractive segments to pursue with the strengths and weaknesses of the branch, and then position the branch for success in the marketplace. Positioning is the task of establishing a viable competitive situation and determining what should be the goals in each market segment. Once the branch positioning has been identified, the marketing mix can be addressed in terms of the product range, pricing, branch and sales-engineering staffing levels, location, stockholding, logistics and publicity.

The mechanism for determining a branch's marketing mix is by constructing a product assessment square that plots market attractiveness against likelihood of success for the range of products available for distribution. Circles are drawn proportional to the size of market available within the territory, with a segment indicating the present market share. A judgment is then made on the relative market attractiveness, in terms of gross margin, and the likelihood of success

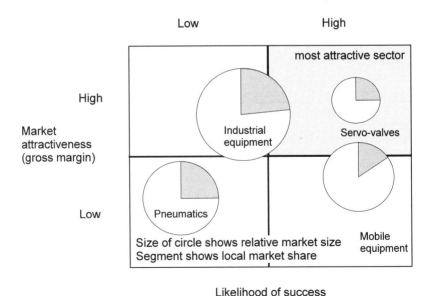

Figure 6.7   Product assessment square

Table 6.3 *Strategic agenda*

Priority	Current position	Action	Intent and targets
Industrial	Main activity < 14% share	Develop local marketing plan	Strengthen leadership > 15%
Maintenance repair & overhaul	Opportunistic < 0.5%	Develop maintenance contracts with major end-users in territory	Attain leadership > 10%
Electro-hydraulics	Opportunistic < 5%	Establish electro-hydraulic expertise and sales programme	Attain leadership > 13%
Power units	Designed by sales < 2%	Local market planning and establish network of expertise	Major player > 3%
Mobile	Low priority < 4%	Assess the market potential and add necessary product lines	Gain market share > 10%
Connectors	Niche < 2%	Sell as a product line for MRO and in systems as required	Additional product
Pneumatic	Existing staff	Continue to sell existing lines and track the market	Add on if attractive

in securing the sale. The position of the circles then shows which product groups offer the greatest sales potential (see Figure 6.7).

Action has then to be taken to position the business in its chosen market segments, and a strategy statement made that defines the priorities, outlines the current position, identifies actions that need to be taken, and the business performance targets that must be achieved. An example from the fluid power industry is shown in Table 6.3. This strategic agenda provides the framework for a branch to use for determining its position in the target market segments. All routine and daily decisions must be in line with this agenda and contribute to repositioning the business. For example:

- All new product lines must increase the overall service level, and have a sales pattern creating the required number of separate demands per year.
- All customers must be identified on a pricing matrix, with confirmation that they are correctly positioned.
- Staff-training requirements must be identified and be progressing, in preparation for selling an expanded product range.
- Sales plans and targets must be established for each segment of the market.
- Budgets must be established for facilities and equipment needed to develop opportunities.
- A plan must be agreed on local advertising, integrating with a national policy.

This completes the main elements for developing a marketing plan. The next phase is to plan the implementation to gain increased sales.

TACTICAL SALES TECHNIQUES

The strategic analysis and marketing plans will only generate increased sales if implemented effectively, which means developing tactical best-practice selling techniques. This requires *prospects* to be converted to *customers* and developed to generate *sales*. Tactical selling addresses:

- Which accounts are the most attractive in terms of gross margin?
- How should the accounts be allocated across the sales-force?
- How should the sales people use their time to greatest effect?
- How often should calls be made to protect, grow or develop accounts?
- How price-sensitive is an account?
- What is the delivery lead-time expected by the customer?
- How is the sales-force measured and motivated?

The sales-force is crucial, acting as the *eyes* and *ears* in the marketplace. Its personnel need to be integrated into the information loop providing regular feedback for the marketing process, and this information must be routinely updated to continually improve the identification of potential customers and a knowledge-base for local markets.

CUSTOMER SELECTION

The key driver of profitability is *gross margin* and a selection process is required for identifying which customers provide the greatest opportunity.

Customer Profiling

Information on customers has to be systematically collected and stored on an electronic database with analysis tools for sorting and generating relevant management reports. The basic information required is:

- Customer details, contact names and position in the organisation;
- Size of business: sales volumes, number of employees;
- Market classification – SIC code, main markets, including key customers;
- Main activities on site, and product lines purchased;
- Spend profile on products distributed by the distributor; and
- Additional services and products they require from a preferred supplier

Customer Classification

Customers need to be classified based upon their potential and actual spend on equipment supplied by the branch. Codes need to be established that determine the attractiveness and priority for each type of customer. These need to be developed at local level reflecting the requirements of the area served.

An example for the fluid power industry in the USA is shown here:

A	< $10 000	Small user within the state, city.
B	$1000–10 000	User with < $10 k potential for all products, typical basic maintenance repair and overhaul (MRO) user.
C	> $10 000	Large MRO user and /or purchaser of hydraulic equipment.
D	< $10 000	Casual re-seller.
E	> $10 000	Fluid power re-seller, competitor, power transmission manufacturer.

F > $10 000   OEM and/or companion distributor in
                   adjacent territory.
G < $10 000   Small OEM or jobbing shop.
H > $10 000   Fluid power repairer/re-builder.
I > $1   Out-of-area small non-companion distributor.

This classification provides a selection process for prospective customers, and allows a cost-effective method of servicing accounts to be
established. Accounts can be serviced in a variety of ways but the
method adopted must reflect and protect the available gross margins.

SALES PLANNING

Account Classification

All accounts need to be validated including prospective customers in
relation to:

- Range of products purchased;
- Likelihood of acquiring business from a competitor;
- Account attractiveness for the branch; and
- Potential level of gross margin.

This can be translated onto a matrix (Figure 6.8) that compares
account attractiveness with the chances of success.
   Account attractiveness is characterised by:

- Size or growth potential;
- Profitability/price sensitivity;
- Order schedule stability and visibility;
- Range of products used;
- Location; and
- Order size.

Chance of success is determined by:

- Compatibility of products available;
- Current market penetration;
- Requirement for dual source; and
- Current relationship and reputation of present supplier.

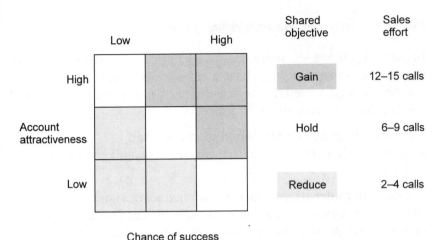

Figure 6.8 Matrix for account classification

It is important to focus sales effort onto accounts which are *attractive* but also have a *high* likelihood of success. (In the previous fluid power example this would mean targeting accounts in the C and F classifications.)

Territorial Structure

Once accounts have been classified they should be allocated to the sales-force based upon:

- Products/industry skills needed to meet the customers' expectations;
- A person's relationship and knowledge of the customer;
- Mix of accounts that needs to be protected or grown;
- Number of visits required to site and location;
- Concentrations of similar businesses in the locality; and
- Competitor presence and market position.

In the industrial distribution business, controlling more than 8 to 10 people can be ineffective, therefore reporting links and structures need to be carefully considered to provide ready access to appropriate technical and sales support.

Price Sensitivity and Matrix Pricing

In general, OEMs are more sensitive to price than other users, but usually most customers purchase a range of products so that prices can be adjusted to reflect the sensitivity of particular products and volume discount structures. In practice:

- Primary lines attract maximum discounts; and
- Secondary lines can be used to increase the overall gross margin for the account.

Using computer-based ordering and invoicing systems, a discount structure by customer and products can be developed providing a *customer-specific price matrix*. These must be used each time an order is placed to optimise the price charged. This information needs to be updated regularly in order to maximise the *gross margin* generated, by the business.

A *small* increase in *price* has a *LARGE* impact upon *profitability*.

SALES ACTION PROCESSES

Influence of Key Buying Factors

Understanding the key buying factors for each customer segment provides the foundation for determining a pricing strategy. An example based upon fluid power equipment is shown in Figure 6.9. Further segmentation is possible by categorising new business, repeat orders, and maintenance repair and overhaul purchases if thought relevant for a particular business or territory.

Account Strategy

Each type of customer needs to be treated differently taking account of:

- Account economics;
- Importance of the customer;
- Key buying factors for the market sector;
- Branch and business objectives for the particular market;
- Products required and the skills needed to engineer the system;
- Local competition; and
- Alternative solutions using different technology.

	OEM	User	Re-seller
Industrial sector	brand price technical support	sales/technical effort brand delivery price	brand delivery customer service
Mobile sector	brand sales/technical effort price delivery		sales effort brand delivery local presence

Figure 6.9 Key buying factors

Generally it is easier to increase market-share by developing current accounts and expanding the range of products and services offered, than to promote new ones.

- Business should be won by providing better service;
- Price reductions should only be used as a last resort;
- The support of the product's manufacturer should be sought wherever possible;
- Supplier rationalisation and the trend to out-source non-critical items should provide further opportunities to supply a wider range of products; and
- Customers look for a family of items packaged ready for use.

SELLING TECHNIQUES

It is important to understand the difference between a complex and a simple safe sale, and to appreciate the additional effort needed to develop new accounts; typically it is three times more difficult than maintaining an existing customer.

Selling is concerned with:

- Recognising the customer's needs;
- Evaluating the options available to satisfy the requirements;
- Resolving and satisfying the customer's concerns;
- Supporting the decision to buy; and
- Selling on *value* rather than price (value = benefit + price).

Several training courses are available for promoting effective selling. One that has gained a reasonable reputation is the SPIN technique by Neil Rackham (1987) for investigating and questioning:

(S)ituation questions	seller obtains information – establishes the purpose of the call.
(P)roblem questions	involvement of the buyer – understanding of the need.
(I)mplication questions	buyer realises there is a problem the seller can solve.
(N)eed/pay off questions	buyer understands the benefit.

Another example used in the UK is the PIRBIC system which seeks to create a selling philosophy within the business, covering the needs of the salespeople and sales managers. Areas explained include:

- Planning time to achieve the most efficient use of available resources;
- Planning territories and targeting where individual salespersons should call;
- Discovering the customers' needs and matching the services to satisfy them;
- Gaining customers' commitment; and
- Understanding the need to close a sale.

Sales managers are taught how to train and coach salespeople using the PIRBIC materials to reinforce good sales practice.

Whatever system is used: inquiries generate quotations, which provide orders, which keep the business in existence.

The effectiveness of the overall process is influenced by the internal salespeople and everybody associated with the team, which means everyone has to use their time striving to make profitable sales.

However, the greatest influence on sales is the time a salesperson spends directly face to face with the customer, and the largest impact upon profitability is by asking the customer when they need delivery. Products required with a long lead-time can be shipped directly from the manufacturer, leaving the branch to collect the cash and take their margin.

SALES-FORCE EFFECTIVENESS

Coaching and Training

Very few companies have a totally effective sales-force, and there is normally a considerable amount of slack in people's actual performance and in underutilised sales potential. A sales-force's effectiveness can be improved by:

- Better deployment of resources (management);
- More effective provision and use of sales support (organisation); and
- Effective selling skills and techniques (training).

Selling skills can be enhanced by recruitment of new people, training existing staff and through coaching. Improvements in these areas lead directly to sustainable higher margins and repeat business (see Figure 6.10). Coaching is a process where managers reinforce classroom training with joint visits and the use of training accounts. Coaching must be developed constructively, focusing on improving selling techniques with clear achievement goals. It also helps to promote the style and behaviour expected of people working for the business. The skills obtained through training alone are quickly lost. If these skills are to be sustained and developed further they must be applied with appropriate coaching support from an experienced manager. It is worth noting that good sales people do not necessarily make good managers!

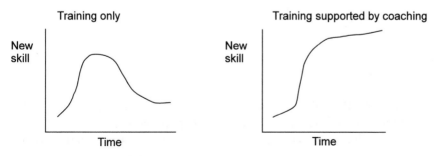

Figure 6.10   The effect of coaching

EVALUATION AND APPRAISAL

Control Systems

The system for controlling the sales-force should be simple to operate and make full use of IT support to minimise the amount of time spent compiling and writing reports. There should be easy ways to collate and analyse information on customers, access to measures of performance, order-tracking and technical data, to increase the effectiveness of the selling process. *Sales people should be fully supported in their prime purpose to SELL and not burdened with complex systems and unnecessary paperwork.*

The relationship between the salesperson and the manager should focus upon the following tasks, with responsibilities and targets established through an appraisal process and progress monitored on a regular basis (see Figure 6.11). The mission and objectives agreed for both regional managers and salespeople should reinforce the need for growth, good account management and effective selling.

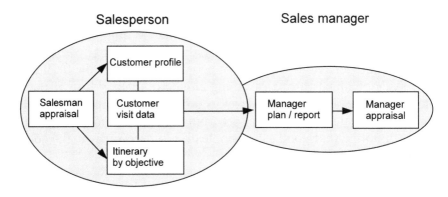

Figure 6.11   The salesperson–sales manager interrelationship

Time Allocation

An analysis of a salesperson's time detailing the time spent facing the customer, travelling, waiting, meetings, paperwork, telephoning and eating lunch alone provides a good illustration of the effective use of time (Table 6.4).

Table 6.4 *Salesperson's time analysis*

	Sales force	Best practice
Lunch alone	8%	5%
Telephone	9%	5–10%
Meetings and paperwork	43%	5–20%
Traveling and waiting	20%	25–35%
Customer *face* time	20%	40–50%

Time spent face to face with the customer is by far the most productive activity for a salesperson to generate sales.

Providing effective sales support can considerably increase sales efficiency allowing more time for salespeople to spend with customers, effectively increasing the size of the sales-force. This can be further enhanced, making more effective use of the time spent with customers by using a structured classification system that focuses visits on accounts with higher sales potential.

MEASURES OF PERFORMANCE (MoP)

Any payment and reward system must reinforce the business strategy and promote the desired behaviour required by the management team, giving consideration to:

- Company strategy;
- Account strategy;
- Coaching and development of the workforce;
- Gross margin generation;
- Gross margin per sales person; and
- New account development.

Therefore the measures of performance and their respective targets need to be qualitative and quantitative in order to drive improved performance combined with reinforcing the strategy.

For example the type of performance measures that needed to be considered are those shown in Table 6.5. Each category can be scored relative to its impact upon the business and people's performance reviewed on a regular basis. Used constructively, these reviews form

Table 6.5 *Performance measures*

Salesperson's MoP	Manager's MoP
Attitude and presentation	Regional sales increase (10%)
Sales call planning	Account prioritisation complete
Sales increase (15%)	Number of sales calls per week
Gross margin generated	Gross margin across the product
Organisation of time and visits	range
Order closure	Salespeople's time facing customers
Inquiry generation	Maintaining the pricing mix
Prospecting for new opportunities	Reports accurate and timely
Acting and following up on	Monthly sales meetings and reports
instructions	Improved service levels
Product knowledge	Innovative thinking
Regular contact with the office	Coaching skills
Actual to planned customer visits	Lost business/accounts
Lost/protected accounts/orders	

the basis for identifying development needs and targets for improvement. Clearly all MoPs have to be carefully considered and tailored to specific types of business, but they must be regularly monitored and supported by an appropriate incentive and reward structure.

Note: 'You get what you measure' and 'what you measure gets done', even if it is not what you want!

Break-even Analysis by Business

A break-even analysis for the total distribution business and each branch is critical when assessing the growth potential. Branches trade within a defined territory and it is important to know the level of sales revenue that must by achieved to cover the cost associated with having an established local branch. Break-even analysis which plots sales revenues against costs, is a proven technique for determining the level of risk to a business's profits due to failing to meet sales targets. The aim for any distribution business is to minimise the fixed costs element, and control all other expenses in proportion to the level of sales.

SUMMARY

This section has identified the main elements needed to manage an industrial distribution business and develop a marketing and sales plan for the business. The fluid power industry in the USA has been used as an example to illustrate the principles, but it is believed that these can be applied to a range industrial products sold to commercial customers. The need for good distribution channels is growing in importance as products are introduced into wider markets. Many manufacturing companies with expertise in product introduction and supply chain management do not have the desire, market size, resources or skills to develop overseas markets. Therefore, they rely upon intermediate distributors to provide the necessary knowledge and local presence needed to trade successfully in these potentially attractive territories. The key to success is having a well trained, motivated sales-force, because they meet the customer, establish the relationships and take the orders. These are vital activities for the supporting the complete supply chain and all business activities involved in an industry.

7

Customer Satisfaction and Quality

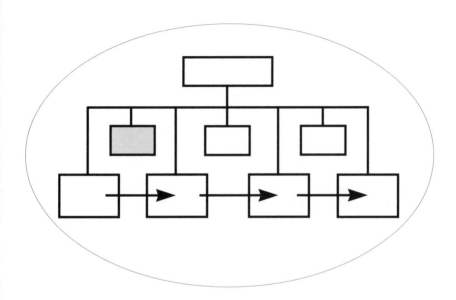

Topics

Introduction
Establishing customer monitors and reporting systems
Customer satisfaction route map
Creating and communicating the vision
Code of ethical conduct
Customer-focused programmes
The quality-improvement process
Safety review board
Formal quality procedures
Statistical methods and process control
Quality-improvement route maps
Performance measures
Summary

7

Customer Satisfaction and Quality

INTRODUCTION

The four fundamental business processes need some staff support operating across the different business areas, directing and integrating activities. One of these roles is customer satisfaction and quality; it is a role not widely employed by companies, but provides the remit for ensuring that regular customer contact is maintained at senior management level. It seeks to understand the customer's perception of how the company is performing as a supplier. It also has the authority within the business to instigate any corrective actions needed to resolve customer problems and has responsibility for ensuring the necessary quality systems are fully-developed and relentlessly followed by everybody associated with providing products and services. This is an extremely broad role, normally assigned the responsibility of an experienced senior manager with a small team providing expertise to initiate and drive projects. The resources needed for implementation remain within the core business processes, to prevent establishing bureaucratic systems that would remove ownership from the managers responsible for delivering the operational objectives.

ESTABLISHING CUSTOMER MONITORS AND REPORTING SYSTEMS

Customer rating systems for assessing a company's supplier performance have been developed and implemented by many original equipment manufacturers for both new and aftermarket products. These *customer performance measures* tend to be based upon *league tables* which are used to determine the relative position of main suppliers in terms of:

- *Quality of items supplied*, using the number of items rejected by the customer's production or aftermarket operations, calculated in terms of parts per million.
- *Delivery of components to schedule*, assessed as the percentage of actual line items delivered against the number ordered, within an agreed time period.
- *Price of goods and services*, cost of ownership relative to other suppliers or the achievement of negotiated cost savings.

The measurement systems tend to be unsophisticated, and weightings placed upon the different factors can vary depending upon the company's preferences. However, if customers do generate information concerning a supplier's performance, no matter how imprecise, then if your company is in the lower half of the vendor's list it is essential that the management team knows and remedial action is taken to resolve the situation. Collating this information from a number of customers provides an internal 'customer measure' that can be used by the management team to monitor trends, highlight good performance and prepare recovery plans for persistent under-achievement. Obtaining a balanced measure is difficult due to inconsistencies in available information, and consequently the task of receiving and interpreting these reports must be undertaken by a senior manager who is independent from operations and able to conduct an informed unbiased assessment.

The other important customer measure is *customer perception*. This is more difficult to quantify, because customers do not formally generate this information on suppliers, but it is critically important to gauge a customer's perception of your company as a supplier. Many views are held within a company concerning the credibility of a supplier, and these opinions influence the relationships that are needed to sustain current contracts and create opportunities on new product introduction programmes. Obtaining a reliable, unbiased, informed view takes considerable effort, but once attained provides a powerful management tool for determining what actions should be taken to protect the share of current business and how to position negotiations on future contracts. One approach that has been used successfully, particularly in the USA, is to employ consultants who specialise in acquiring this type of information. In some instances they solicit the customer's views without identifying the company, in order to obtain an unbiased opinion, particularly on price. The disadvantage of using consultants is that the business receives the customer's comments secondhand after a degree of interpretation. A more satisfactory method, if it can be established, is for the manager responsible for customer satisfaction and quality to work with the major customers to obtain their considered opinion on the following attributes:

- *Communication* – how well does the company communicate its intentions, keeping all levels of management informed, using both formal and informal methods of communication?
- *Commercial* – how competitive are the products and services on price and overall cost of ownership?
- *Equipment* – how does the equipment perform in service, meeting the specified performance criteria, with a service life well beyond the warranty period?
- *Technical* – how technically advanced are the products relative to the competition, and does the company have access to the next generation of technical innovation?
- *Support* – how well does the company respond to problems that occur in development programmes and products in service?

Each area can be scored over a range of, say, six points and an average value calculated to provide an overall quantified assessment:

1 Unsatisfactory performance, remedial action needed.
2 Poor performance, causing concern to the customer.
3 Adequate performance, tolerated by the customer.
4 Average performance, accepted by the customer.
5 Good performance, meets the customer's expectation.
6 Outstanding performance, exceeds the customer's expectation.

The goal is to exceed the customer's expectation, and delight the customer: however, most businesses find their actual performance is far short of this ideal. Customer satisfaction assessments need to be spaced at regular intervals giving sufficient time for corrective actions to be reflected in the scores, because once a company has been made aware of its particular shortcomings, then the customer expects management action to be taken resulting in an improved level of performance.

CUSTOMER SATISFACTION ROUTE MAP

The introduction of customer satisfaction measures tends to reveal a number of shortcomings that need to be addressed. A method of systematically transforming the business from mediocre performance relative to product consistency, customer support and problem resolution, into a company respected for the quality of its products, and recognised for effective interactive customer support, is through the development and implementation of a customer satisfaction route map as shown in Figure 7.1.

The management team for businesses should construct such a map and identify any shortcomings that exist within customer relationships, based upon an initial customer satisfaction survey and assessment. Three factors that must be remembered are:

1. It is easier to keep and grow existing customers than to develop new ones.
2. The customer's perception – no matter how unjust – is reality.
3. A viable business cannot be sustained without satisfied customers.

The techniques used to improve customer satisfaction are founded upon delivering quality-assured products or services, and any deficiencies must be identified and immediately rectified in collaboration with the customer. However, several initiatives can be taken to improve the overall performance of the company, raising workforce awareness of the importance of satisfying customers.

CREATING AND COMMUNICATING THE VISION

The company business plan details the role of the business and defines the challenges facing it. These plans take considerable effort to assemble, but once prepared businesses tend to keep the information confidential to senior managers. If the workforce is to understand the business and how to support its customers, then the manager responsible for customer satisfaction should create a summarised version of the plan, maintaining the confidentiality of sensitive information but providing the workforce and customers with a full appreciation of the company's goals and objectives.

One effective way of communicating these objectives and making everyone aware of the challenges facing the business, linked to the magnitude of the change needed to remain competitive, is through

Areas	Factors	Strategic issues	Deliverables
Product consistency	Implement PIM process Use quality assured suppliers Define manufacturing routes Confirm process capability ISO 9000 quality system Meet delivery promises	Team-working culture Shared company vision Agreed goals & objectives Customer-orientated teams Customer-focused actions Self-directed teams	Consistent fulfilment of commitments
Formal verification	Review performance monitors Conduct management audits Maintain quality records Review product safety record Introduce ethics programme Open contract management	Employee commitment Visible professionalism Personal development Skills training Career progression Payment and rewards	Shared trust and confidence Employees proud of products
Visible deliverables	Improved business image Enthusiastic employees Reduction in defects Improved documentation	Organisational flexibility Quality the top priority Measures of performance Product integrity	Individuals care for customers
Customer awareness	Awareness of customers' needs Formal perception monitors Good two-way communication Common goals and values	Customer-focused training Ethics programmes Process capability training Team-building events	Prompt service for customers
Company orientation	Achievement-based culture Failure-prevention attitudes Flexible supportive workforce Continual improvement ethic Customer valued by everyone	Quality-improvement plan Team-selection process User-friendly documents Consistent record of events	Delighted customers

Figure 7.1 Customer satisfaction route map

giving a concise presentation to the workforce and later displaying it prominently in an accessible chart-room. The type of information that should be shared includes:

- An outline of the parent company's strategy, identifying areas for growth and the position of the particular businesses within the overall company.
- The strategic direction for the business.
- A simple vision statement encapsulating the goals and ambitions of the business and relevance to the workforce.
- Strategic objectives identifying how the business must be positioned in its chosen markets.
- Global industry trends with a statement of factors that will impact the company.
- Market drivers detailing the features customers want, and will pay for, including opportunities to extend the range of products and services purchased.
- A product plan identifying the key product introduction projects and possible opportunities.
- A vision on how the business must improve operational effectiveness.
- Operational targets that must be achieved to remain competitive and maintain the customer-base.
- Concepts on how the business processes should be structured.
- The process for implementing change projects.
- Outline plans of significant change projects established by the business.
- The key values for the business detailing important management principles, that is,
  - be sure the *customer* comes first,
  - joint responsibility through improved decision-making,
  - team performance more important than individual effort,
  - people must meet commitments, and
  - integrity in all business activities.
- Leadership values identifying the management style, that is,
  - pride in team performance,
  - mutual trust,
  - lead by example,
  - encourage people to take reasonable calculated risks, and
  - say thank you and mean it.

The management team must give considerable thought to establishing and deciding to declare key values and leadership values. These can be openly discussed with the workforce and then a value statement signed by everyone to demonstrate acceptance. Personal experience has shown them to be a powerful tool in gaining people's confidence for accepting change, but they must be implicitly followed to avoid feelings of betrayal when events make them difficult to keep.

The chart-room concept that displays information about the company, together with the status of the major projects that are critical to the future success of the business, is an effective mechanism for making people aware of the issues facing the business. This open access approach answers many queries and allows people to identify with the challenges that need to be addressed. It also provides an excellent way of informing visitors about the company, and initiatives being taken to secure a future for the business.

CODE OF ETHICAL CONDUCT

Codes of ethical conduct are being developed by many companies, and it is important to establish the conduct that the company expects from all its employees. Unethical conduct is not necessarily motivated by personal gain and often results from a mistaken belief that one is benefiting the company. A series of statements covering the following aspects should be prepared in the form of an instruction booklet, and key messages on ethical behaviour prominently displayed on posters throughout the business. The booklet should address:

- Applicability of the code and the people to whom it applies.
- Compliance with the code, providing guidance and understanding of the types of activity in which the company will *not* participate.
- The purpose and role of a business ethics committee:
  - provides training in the code of ethical conduct,
  - agrees unacceptable standards of conduct,
  - oversees the training of all employees in business ethics,
  - ensures employees are asked to sign the code, acknowledging they have received training, and that they understand and will abide by the code, and
  - monitors the results of investigations and approves the resolution of alleged incidents.

- The appointment of a company ethics officer to

  ○ coordinate committee activities,
  ○ monitor a company 'hotline' which can be used in strict confidence to report alleged violations, and
  ○ instigate an investigation and resolution of any reported violation.

- Personal conflicts of interest that may arise.
- Bribes, gifts, gratuities and entertainment *never* being used or received for gaining competitive advantage. A statement should be made on what gifts, gratuities and entertainment, if any, may be accepted.
- Accuracy of records and accounts ensuring all transactions are properly authorised.
- Critical aspects of government laws and regulations.
- Violation of reporting procedures and the company's expectation from employees.
- Disciplinary action to be taken by the company for violation of the code.
- Personal signatures acknowledging employees understand the code.

The introduction of codes of ethics is particularly relevant when trading with government agencies; in some countries the penalties for violation have cost companies millions of pounds in fines and debarment from future programmes.

The management time involved in developing an ethics programme is considerable and once implemented must be maintained with the highest integrity. Codes of ethical conduct have been adopted by major suppliers to the United States of America Department of Defense, and indications are that companies in other industries across the world are introducing similar codes.

CUSTOMER-FOCUSED PROGRAMMES

The concept of everyone being involved in providing customer service, not just the people who have direct contact with the customer, is not readily understood. People working in the supply chain need to be introduced to this way of thinking and understand that they are also suppliers and customers to each other. One method of spreading this knowledge is through using a training company specialising in providing customer-focused training. The process is initiated by everyone completing a questionnaire. Information is collated and analysed to assess people's current level of understanding on customer-related topics. For instance:

- What are people's goals at work?
- Which activities are they responsible for?
- What is the difference between effectiveness and efficiency?
- Which forms of communication are used?
- How important are communication and working relationships between teams?
- Who are the major customers and what is their customer relationship?
- What is the meaning of customer service and how does it impact financial success?
- How aware is the team of quality and how seriously is it taken?
- How well-understood is the need for changes?
- How committed is everybody to keeping agreements and striving to succeed?
- How are people recognised and rewarded for effort?
- How committed are people to satisfying customers?
- Is teamwork effective?
- How aware are people of the business vision and the present financial position?

The questions are constructed to elicit honest opinions; the answers provide the focus for subsequent customer-awareness training. This is normally delivered to large mixed groups of employees, and is based upon a bespoke set of pre-developed modules and exercises that address the issues and shortcomings identified by the initial questionnaire. A typical range of topics may be:

- What is meant by customer service and the impact of different levels of service.
- How to identify 'winners and losers'.
- Determining a person's aim in life and motivation for advancement.
- The thinking process and how to release untapped potential.
- The infinite capacity of the brain and techniques to apply its power.

- Building relationships and determining which are important.
- Acknowledgment and praise for the individual.
- Coping with stress and being aware of its impact upon your life.
- Non-verbal communication through body-language and personal presentation.
- Communicating with people, understanding relationships and feelings.
- Dealing with aggressive people and being assertive.
- Creating a positive attitude to life leading to greater opportunity.
- Basic attitudes and the relationship with customer service.
- The importance of time when delivering customer service.

The result of people attending a customer-focused course is the creation of a new awareness and enthusiasm for what is needed to provide customer service. However, for the company to benefit from the training programme, improvement team leaders have to be appointed and trained in methods that will deliver tangible improvements in customer service. Therefore, the next phase is to form such teams and establish action plans for the areas of customer service the company must address. The mechanism for change should be based upon a team approach, using the disciplines of good project management. Topics may include:

- Identifying personal contacts and the service expected by customers;
- Satisfying the customer's expectation;
- Improving core and peripheral services leading to enhanced customer loyalty;
- Handling customer complaints and recovery strategies;
- Relationships with internal customers and ways of improving performance;
- Management styles and the need for coaching;
- Holding positive, constructive meetings;
- Establishing commitments and delivering promises; and
- Implementing a team's recommendations and taking ownership.

The benefits of this training should be reflected in the customer performance measures and the improved relationships that are developed with both internal and external customers. Some businesses have derived significant commercial benefit from having developed a greater awareness of the need to provide good customer service, and this type of initiative should be given serious consideration when the company's customer perception is tarnished.

THE QUALITY-IMPROVEMENT PROCESS

The foundation of customer satisfaction is supplying on time, quality products that exceed the customer's expectation. New products, developed using a product introduction process structured around multidisciplinary teams taking responsibility for simultaneously designing products and supply chain processes, should be robust, high-quality products when they enter the market. However, the majority of products in the company's portfolio may not have been subject to this type of rigorous process and consequently may be prone to greater variability in quality. Therefore a quality-improvement process is required, that gathers information from products in service and analyses the results to determine what actions need to be taken to improve in-service performance (Figure 7.2). Collecting such information is essential because it provides the understanding necessary to respond to customers' requirements, and allows corrective action to be taken in anticipation of future events. It also identifies the critical features important to the customer which must be incorporated into new designs.

The quality improvement process is owned by the customer satisfaction and quality team and should be established as a formal review process that meets, say, *monthly*, attended by the management team responsible for the design maintenance and product manufacture. Products with a persistently unsatisfactory performance record should be documented, and escalated to higher management giving them visibility of actions being taken to resolve outstanding problems.

Benefits from having a formal quality-improvement process based upon the record of products in service are:

- Improved robustness of products in service, increasing durability;
- Reduced cost of failure to the company, customer and ultimate owner;
- Reduced risk of expensive product replacement programmes;
- Improved relationships with the customer, listening and being proactive in identifying and resolving problems;

212

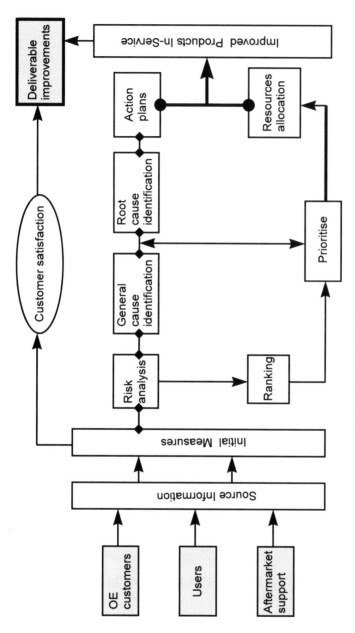

Figure 7.2 Quality-improvement process

- A formal process for assessing risk and implementing corrective actions in place;
- Established routine performance assessment system for seeking information on products in service;
- Important in-service performance information needed for the product introduction process collected;
- Continuous improvement process for current products created;
- In-service performance of products can be measured, monitored and action taken to eliminate failure and minimise risk of litigation; and
- Reduced cost of product ownership and increased customer satisfaction.

The introduction of formal methods for monitoring in-service performance is standard practice with original equipment manufacturers. The collection of similar information for component and system suppliers is more difficult, although several companies, particularly in the automotive sector, are seeking ways to implement in-service quality systems as a mechanism for focusing management resolve to improve product reliability and form closer relationships with customers.

SAFETY REVIEW BOARD

If the products being manufactured are to be used in safety-critical applications, or the service record of products is inferior to major competitors, then the company should establish a safety review board. This board, chaired by the manager of customer satisfaction and quality, comprises senior managers appointed for their knowledge, experience and authority. It is given mandatory power to resolve any issue related to product safety and integrity. The group meets on a regular basis to formally review all incidents or accidents that have legal implications, or potential to seriously damage the company's reputation. The senior person and key team members responsible for the product or process that has caused the incident are ordered to attend and present the salient facts of the occurrence and proposed corrective actions deemed necessary to resolve the problem. The minutes of the meeting are accurately recorded, and action resulting from the review released together with the authority needed to implement the recommendations. The meeting is also attended by the company's legal representative and, when appropriate, third-party insurance agents.

FORMAL QUALITY PROCEDURES

The ISO 9000 series of standards is concerned with establishing a system of quality management within the organisation, allowing customers to evaluate suppliers and compare their potential to meet acceptable levels of quality and reliability. The principle of the standard is based upon formalising processes and standardising the approach for achieving quality, not the detailed activities that underpin the process. Several advantages result from having ISO accreditation:

- Customers want to deal with accredited companies;
- Increased marketing advantage from being known as a quality-approved supplier;
- Meeting an industrial sector requirement, being ISO approved to win orders;
- Improving the control of processes needed to achieve business objectives; and
- Providing formal documentation regarding people's responsibilities and authority.

Therefore in the competitive global marketplace, viable companies need a formal quality system, normally based upon ISO 9000, aimed at improving quality, reducing quality costs and improving customer confidence.

Requirements of the Standard

The basic requirements are to identify those elements of the business process that have an impact upon product quality or service, and to establish documented procedures that ensure operational consistency in a planned manner. ISO 9001 is the most stringent standard in the series and covers the following areas:

- A formal statement from the managing director on the business objectives, linked to a policy statement on quality and its importance to the company, and a formal quality system is written for the following business processes:

Customer Development Process
- Identifying the opportunity for developing new products;
- Evaluating market requirements to satisfy the business objectives;
- Obtaining product and project approval to submit a proposal;
- Winning the order and gaining board approval;

Product Introduction Process
- Developing the product and process design;
- Validating the concept, culminating in product release using production tooling;
- Implementing the supply-chain process, leading to product launch;
- Manufacturing support needed for increasing output to meet customers' schedules;

Supply-chain Management
- Purchasing control, ensuring products conform to specified requirements;
- Identification of products and traceability, linking products to specifications;
- Control of manufacturing processes with work instructions and procedures;
- Control of specialist processes, including environmental requirements;
- Methods for inspection and testing product conformance including

  - receiving inspection and supplier quality assurance,
  - in-process monitoring and control,
  - product monitoring and conformance verification,
  - final inspection and performance testing, and
  - inspection test records and documentation;

- Inspection of measuring and test equipment, calibration, capability and condition;
- Methods of inspection and recording the test status of products in the factory;
- Control of non-conforming products and methods of identification;
- Corrective actions to rectify defects;
- Handling, storage and delivering products to customers;

- Quality records and methods of retrieving and controlling information;
- Internal quality audit procedures;
- Training requirements and skills needed for operating to the quality procedures.

The control of documentation is a critical aspect of the ISO quality process, and:

- All documents must be approved and authorised prior to release;
- The actual issue in use must be current and systematically updated;
- Any obsolete documents must be removed to prevent possible error;
- Changes to the product, process or procedures must be formally recorded; and
- The latest issue of a document must be easily identified and available for use.

The preparation of formal *quality procedures* is a considerable task, particularly when taking account of the training required to make the workforce comply with procedures. When writing them it is essential to involve the people who will implement and use the procedures. The audit process verifies that procedures are being followed implicitly, and if written in a bureaucratic style implementation can be extremely difficult. To gain accreditation, the system must be audited by an approved third-party agent who confirms the procedures are being applied correctly.

The responsibility of the customer satisfaction team is to provide guidance and support for the preparation of the quality system documentation and to conduct regular internal audit reviews to verify the system is being rigorously followed.

STATISTICAL METHODS AND PROCESS CONTROL

The application of statistical methods to confirm the capability and repeatability of processes including measuring systems is paramount to achieving consistent quality. The automotive industry adopted these methods several years ago, but some companies have still to understand the importance of knowing the capability of processes. Factors that are crucial for consistent quality are as follows:

Machine Capability

Machine capability studies demonstrate the ability of the equipment to repeat a process within specified tolerances. The established methods for demonstrating such a capability are:

- By measuring the key characteristics for a number of machined components (ideally a sample greater than 40) without making adjustments, plotting the spread of tolerances due to variations in the machine, material or tooling and using standard routines to calculate the capability.
- By obtaining a manufacturer's machine inspection report giving detailed information on wear in slide-ways, spindles, alignment of axes and concentricity of rotating elements.
- By using pre-control charts to verify that five components can all be made within 50 per cent of the total tolerance band. This technique demonstrates the process is incapable unless all five are within tolerance (quick method developed by Peter Shainin and described in Bhote (1987)).

If the machine is not capable of machining to the required level of process capability, then only four management choices are available:

1. Relax the tolerances on the drawing or material specification.
2. Repair or refurbish the machine.
3. Buy a new machine that is capable of manufacturing to drawing.
4. Manufacture the item using a different process/out-source

Process Capability

The process capability combines the capability of the machine with the skill of the operator and shows how much a particular process, or product parameter is varying during production. The common measure referred to as Cpk indicates the process variation and its relationship to the mean of the specification. A number is calculated using the standard formula; the higher the number the more capable the process (a capability greater than 1.33 should be the target figure).

The methods for verifying process capability include:

- Statistical process control charts that monitor the trend of key characteristics over a period of time. The information is obtained by taking a number of samples at calculated intervals, recording the range of dimensions and plotting the median value against upper and lower control limits.
- Pre-control charts using red, amber and green to annotate and monitor variations of key characteristics against a factor of time intervals between stoppages (simplified control chart technique developed by Peter Shainin).
- Computer-based systems using electronic measuring devices to log information, automatically generate process control charts and provide information on the capability of the process.

Process Capability of Measuring Systems

The capability of the measuring system has a significant impact upon the overall capability of the process, and should be an order of magnitude more precise than the tolerances being measured. The suitability of measuring systems are confirmed by:

- Gauge repeatability and reproducibility (R&R) studies confirming the accuracy and repeatability of the measuring system for the parameters being measured.
- Isoplots using two measurements taken from several components; capability is confirmed if the parameters fall with defined boundaries (Peter Shainin technique).

Deficiencies in the measuring system are significant because they erode the available processing tolerance and are generally less expensive to correct than process deficiencies.

The purpose of machine capability studies and statistical process control is to verify the consistency of the process. These techniques have only limited use for identifying the cause of the problem and corrective actions are needed to improve the process. Therefore, if process capability is to be improved then an action log should be established recording faults, results from experiments designed to identify problems, and the corrective actions taken to improve the robustness of the process.

QUALITY-IMPROVEMENT ROUTE MAPS

All companies have opportunities for improvement. The range of initiatives that could be undertaken normally far exceeds the resources available, and therefore the task of senior management is to identify and promote those projects that have the greatest impact upon *customer satisfaction, quality* and *business operational performance*. Work undertaken preparing a satisfactory business case should have identified benchmark performance targets that need to be achieved to remain competitive in international markets. The purpose of the route map is to identify significant elements of the process than must be improved in order to move from current performance to world class. The recommended approach is shown in Figures 7.3 and 7.4.

The route map is constructed by determining the factors that are crucial to supplying quality projects on time. The current performance is measured and provides an initial starting point; the elements of operational performance that have an impact upon the crucial factors are listed; and the routes linking the different aspects drawn to identify the direct relationships between activities leading to the benchmark performance. In the example of Figure 7.4 the links only demonstrate how a route map might be constructed. The important aspect of the chart is to show the interrelationships between the

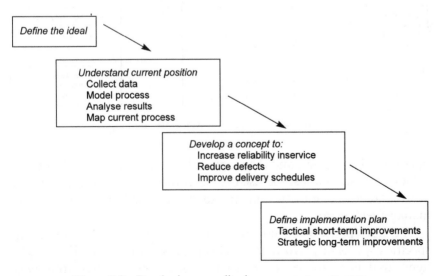

Figure 7.3 Developing a quality-improvement route map

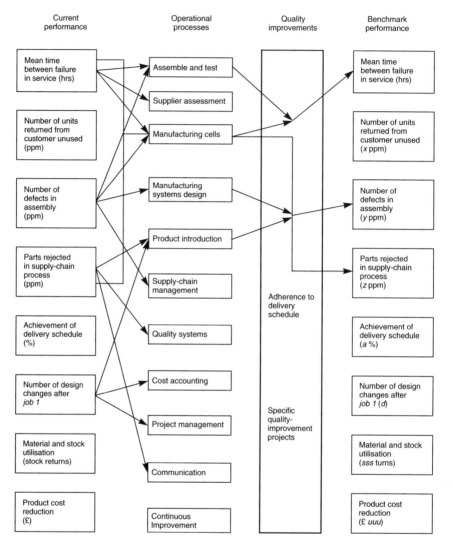

Figure 7.4   Quality-improvement route map

operational processes, and the magnitude of the change that has to be achieved. It should also be used to determine and agree which items are regarded as priority and are to be assigned resources by the management team.

The next phase is to construct route maps aimed at improving specific aspects of performance. This process should identify the key items that need to be addressed to deliver the required improved performance. For example improving adherence to delivery schedules from a current performance of, say, 80 per cent to a benchmark performance of 99 per cent would be achieved using the route map of Figure 7.5 to define the core activities and associated project work packages.

Once the route map has been constructed, the next stage is to define quality-improvement projects with long and short-term objectives. These need to be supported by a time-phased project plan including the resources needed to complete the various work packages. Once approved, the design and implementation should be assigned to a multidisciplinary team of full and part-time members under the day-to-day control of a project manager. Implementing change projects requires considerable resources if the benefits are to be realised in an acceptable time-frame. Therefore, senior management must develop the range of activities focusing effort onto those projects providing genuine customer satisfaction and long-term security for the company and its stakeholders.

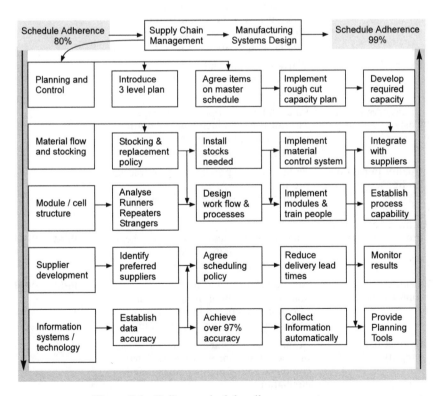

Figure 7.5 Delivery-schedule adherence route map

Table 7.1 *Performance measures*

Customer satisfaction and quality measures	Definition of measure	Performance	
		Current	Target
Customer measures	An assessment made by the manager of customer satisfaction based upon returns from original equipment manufacturers and customers related to quality, delivery and price performance		
Customer perception	A calculated figure based upon the customers' perceptions and assessment of communication, commercial, equipment, technical and support		
Cost of quality Failure costs	The burden of not performing work right first time	£	£
Internal	Costs associated with scrap and rectification, including both labour and materials. Also the proportion of product introduction costs needed to modify designs after *job 1*	£	£
External	Warranty claims and costs of rectification including product substitution programmes		
Quality Assurance Costs	Financial cost of operating the quality assurance system including calibration, process capability, preparation of documentation and training	£	£
Quality Impact on Profit	Failure costs expressed as % of trading profit	%	%
	Failure costs expressed as % of sales	%	%
Technical compliance Product quality	Number of new units rejected by the customer over units dispatched (expressed in parts/million)	PPM	PPM
Product conformance	Achievement of right first-time manufacture – monitoring the number of concessions raised in production compared to number of units shipped	PPM	PPM
Product data integrity	Monitor the outstanding manuals and instruction documents to be updated compared to the number current and in circulation	%	%

Customer satisfaction and quality measures	Definition of measure	Performance	
		Current	Target
Technical compliance (*cont.*)			
Product design	Monitors the effectiveness of product introduction and compares the number of acceptable design changes as a proportion of the total changes after *job 1*. Acceptable changes are customer requests, improved manufacturability, enhanced product performance above specification, negating non-availability of materials/obsolescence	%	%
Commercial compliance			
Delivery to schedule	Measures the achievement of items delivered on time to meet agreed customer schedules. Separate figures may be required for original equipment, aftermarket and repairs	%	%
Delivery lead-time	Measures the average time between receiving an order and the time taken to deliver to the customer	days	days
Turnaround time	Time taken to repair units returned from service, or replacement units needed for production	days	days
Process capability			
Machine capability	Percentage of machines known to have a process capability index of 1.33 or greater compared to the machine population	%	%
Measurement capability	Percentage of measuring systems used to measure key characteristics known to be accurate to less than 5% of the product variation	%	%
Other processes	Percentage of other critical processes controlled using charting procedures for monitoring key characteristics within specified tolerances over time	%	%
Training			
Quality procedures	Average time spent training on customer satisfaction and quality-related subjects per month	hr	hr

PERFORMANCE MEASURES

The mechanism for underpinning customer satisfaction and quality improvements is to establish targets for a series of performance measures that are collected, and reported to senior management on a regular basis. The measures must be readily available without requiring additional clerical support to collect, and be information that is needed to run the business effectively. The parameters to be monitored must encapsulate all aspects of customer satisfaction and be precisely defined to prevent possible misinterpretation across different locations.

A typical set of performance measures are listed in Table 7.1. This list of measures needs tailoring to satisfy differing company requirements, but the discipline of having to routinely measure and report actual performance against agreed targets ensures that managers responsible for delivering customer service and quality keep a focus on this vital activity.

SUMMARY

Customer satisfaction and quality is the foundation for growing a successful business. Combining these two activities is not commonplace in many organisations, but companies that have introduced a senior manager responsible for understanding customer issues with the authority to make necessary changes to the product or service provided have established considerable competitive advantage. The range of initiatives that can be introduced to improve customer awareness and overall quality is very extensive, and all have been shown to provide real business benefits to particular companies. The management effort and resources needed to implement these initiatives and obtain the necessary changes in customer perception must not be underestimated. Therefore the senior management team must decide the priorities for the business and focus its effort into a structured programme that will provide the greatest short and long-term security for the business.

8

Project Management

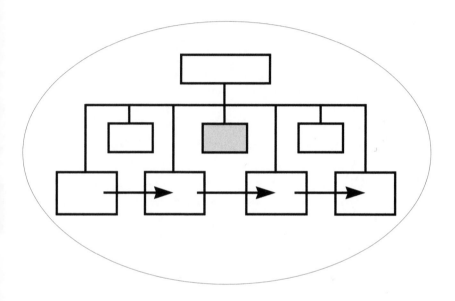

Topics

Introduction
The change process
Project management
Formal project management procedures
Resource-planning and cost-estimating
Project control
Project reporting
Risk management
Hazard reports
Change control
The role of the project manager
Summary

8

Project Management

INTRODUCTION

Project management is a key role needed to support the four fundamental business processes. The overall project manager, often referred to as the programme director, is responsible for ensuring that significant initiatives in customer development, product introduction, supply-chain management, and distribution processes are planned, supported by adequate resources and deliver the agreed benefits. This coordinating activity is normally assigned to a small team of experienced project managers capable of linking initiatives across different business activities, national or international locations. In most instances, project managers become experienced in specific business processes and prefer to manage similar activities. However, the project manager must be accountable to several managers or directors – the project owner, the business process manager who owns the resources, and the programme director with overall responsibility for delivering projects on time and within committed budgets. This group then forms the core steering group, taking overall ownership of the project.

THE CHANGE PROCESS

Change in most businesses is a continual process and must become the normal way of operating for long-term survival. The role of the programme director is to formulate policies and identify step-changes in business performance needed to satisfy all the stakeholders in the business. Projects can be directed towards providing continual improvements to customer satisfaction, quality, increasing the product range or operational performance improvements aimed at restructuring the business. Introducing a step-change in performance may involve:

- Expansion of the product range, requiring significant investment in new facilities;
- Consolidation of businesses and operations;
- Acquisition and disposal of product lines and facilities;
- Relocation of businesses into more appropriate premises;
- Reorganisation of departments and re-structuring around key business processes;
- Introduction of new manufacturing systems, revolutionising working practices;
- Changing the business culture; and/or
- Introduction of new systems and information technology support tools.

All projects have to be assessed in terms of the resource requirement, and priorities established based upon which are regarded as being strategically important for developing the business, forming part of the company's business plan. The business planning process ensures that operational performance improvements, new product introduction programmes, continuous improvement projects and associated operational performance targets are mutually agreed by the senior management team. The terms of reference and the project plans then formalise the commitment to deliver the business objectives and achieve the planned business results.

The initial task is to define the overall change process and identify how it impacts the stakeholders (see Figure 8.1). Customers expect cost-effective products that exceed their expectations, with assurance that the company will continue to provide those products and services in the future. Suppliers require an ongoing reliable customer who encourages open two-way communication and acts with integrity. Employees strive for a secure, stimulating environment that creates opportunity for career advancement, while participating in a team's achievement in developing a successful business. Capital investors expect a secure investment that generates substantial dividends, combined with business growth at a rate that exceeds the increase in the GDP.

Satisfying the stakeholder's requirements is dependent upon two critical factors:

1. Developing and maintaining satisfied customers that are committed to the company; and
2. The business delivering the operational performance committed to the main board.

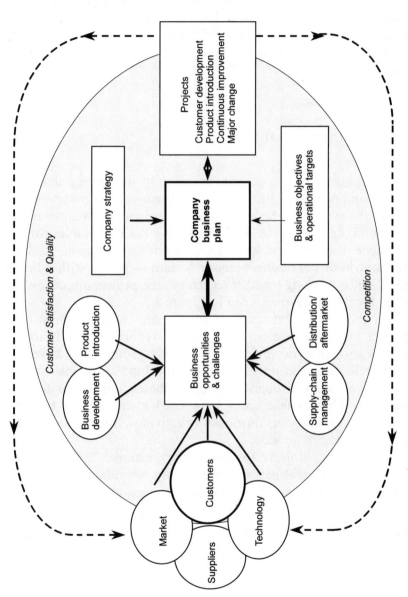

Figure 8.1 The change process

The mechanism for delivering change is based upon developing a *business plan* as described in Chapter 2, which reconciles the influences of the market, prime customers, new technology, major competitors and key suppliers with the company's *vision* and *business objectives*. This leads to a number of business challenges that must be converted into key projects with assigned project owners responsible for exploiting the business opportunities.

PROJECT MANAGEMENT

Project management is a primary mechanism for driving change in products and processes throughout the business. It is fundamental to defining the size of the task, establishing the resource requirements, determining key milestones and identifying the deliverables for the investment. Projects that have a significant impact upon the long term survival of the business require a team of people with a broad base of skills, working together to achieve the project objectives. An outline for the process is shown in Figure 8.2.

Experience shows that for projects to be successful they must have a project owner designated as champion, reporting directly to the management team or review group. This group must have the authority to steer the project, making the funds available for the project to progress through the project phases and deliver the key milestones. These phase gates have been identified for business development and product introduction activities, forming an integral part of the business process.

Major change projects for improving customer satisfaction or enhancing operational performance require a similar approach. To be successful, the following aspects need to be addressed:

- Obtain management agreement on the magnitude of performance improvements needed to be competitive in world markets, using established benchmarks.
- Appoint a senior manager who has direct commitment as project owner.
- Establish project plans that must be implemented as a key element of the business planning process.

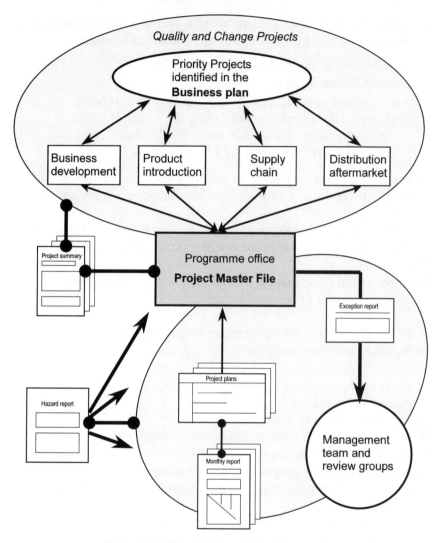

Figure 8.2 The project management process

- Appoint a programme director responsible for owning the process and driving change projects across the business processes and operating units.
- Establish an open system of two-way communication that ensures everyone in the organisation is aware of the challenges facing the business, and the magnitude of the step-change needed to be competitive in global markets.

- Create an accessible chart-room that displays the business goals identified by the business planning process, to include:
  - an outline of the company's strategy;
  - vision for the future;
  - roles of the organisation within the overall company;
  - strategic challenges that are facing the business; and
  - top-level project plans that meet the business objectives, with time-scales for delivering the key milestones.

- Specify a project management planning and control system with an outline procedure of how the project management process will be operated.
- Select a project management software package that supports the process and standardises the documentation used for planning and control.
- Agree criteria for raising *hazard* reports that alert management's attention to the project deliverable at risk.

In my experience, for major projects identified in the business plan to be successful they must have the following:

- A senior manager as owner, with responsibility for exploiting the project deliverables;
- A full-time project manager;
- A detailed project plan with objectives, deliverables, agreed time-scales and resource requirements;
- A team area with project plans on display;
- A core of full-time team members complemented by part-time specialists;
- External support to provide breadth, challenging existing practice and recommending possible alternative solutions;
- A senior management approval and review process that agrees the plan, monitors progress and releases expenditure; and
- A method of tracking progress, reporting expenditure and achievements against delivering key milestones.

FORMAL PROJECT MANAGEMENT PROCEDURES

All projects should be subject to an initial approval process that requires the project manager to prepare a number of standard documents summarising significant aspects of the project. This information is required at a proposal acceptance review and includes a project summary, and planning documents. These should be formally agreed and signed off by the management review group responsible for steering the work and exploiting the deliverables.

The project summary should provide the information shown in Table 8.1.

Table 8.1 *Project summary*

Business	Project title		Project number
Customer	Issue number	Date	Original issue date
Project owner	Project manager		Project classification

Project objectives

Quantified deliverables

It should also provide a project overview that records a baseline for key parameters:

Start date	Completion date	Resources (man months)	Project costs	Capex/ tooling	Pay back (months)

- *Project costs* represent the revenue expenditure for the complete project.
- *Capex* is the capital expenditure required on plant and equipment including tooling over the entire project.
- *Pay back* is the period in months from the start of the project to the point of neutral cumulative cash, that is, the break-even point for the project.

This should be supported by a *financial plan* that establishes the phased expenditures and returns that are expected for the project (Table 8.2). The financial summary can be structured to suit either product introduction or change projects, providing visibility on the level of expenditure and impact on business performance. The financial year identifies the time period; project costs are the non-recurring revenue expenditures including labour, materials and overheads that are required to complete the work packages within the time periods; capital expenditure identifies all the capital expenditure required in the particular time period; and customer contributions and grants shows the funding available from outside the company.

Sales includes the incremental product sales resulting from the project; savings are the benefits that are derived from a substitute product or more effective manufacturing process; PBIT impact is the income from the project contributing to business profitability; cash impact is the difference between the cash generated and the cash consumed by the project; and other business benefits should describe and quantify additional factors such as lead-time reduction, improved customer satisfaction and so forth that are important to the business when monitoring achievements.

Table 8.2 *Financial plan for a project*

Financial year								
Quarter/half	Q1	Q2	Q3	Q4	H1	H2	H3	H4
Project costs (non-recurring) Capital expenditure/tooling Customer contribution/grants Project costs Capital expenditure/tooling								
Sales Savings PBIT impact Cash impact								
Other business benefits								

A project approval mechanism is also required. This requires a project to be formally reviewed and signed off by the appropriate senior managers, signifying the project has been sanctioned to proceed within the agreed expenditure levels:

Approved by	*Name*	*Signature*	*Date*
Managing director			
General manager			
Programme manager			
Project manager			

The *project summary* information should be reviewed at all management reviews throughout the duration of the project and be supported by a current *project plan* that provides a time-phased description of the work-packages, key milestones and resource requirements. Several software packages have been developed to assist in preparing and maintaining project information. These can be extremely useful for planning and monitoring progress (Figure 8.3 for example).

The time-phased project plans also require additional management information for identification and keeping track of achievements:

Business	Project title			Plan agreed
Customer	Project number	Classification	Sheet of	
Project owner	Issue number	Date	Original issue date	
Programme manager	Currency £			

The other essential information is project *milestones.* These should coincide with the major reviews identified by the customer development and product introduction processes and significant events included in the company business plan. Additional milestones may also be added to highlight critical stages to delivering the project on time and within budget. Milestones should be listed as a series of key dates, and used to monitor progress towards achieving these deliverables.

236

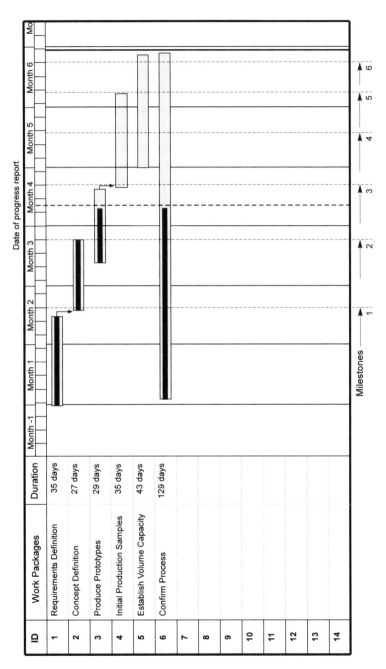

The black line shows progress towards completing the work package and is updated at each project review

Figure 8.3 Outline project plan (Microsoft projects)

The project plan may need further analysis to determine more detailed work schedules, using similar time-based planning charts. This enables the actual resource requirements to be determined and skilled people identified for the project.

RESOURCE-PLANNING AND COST-ESTIMATING

This is one of the most difficult tasks for the project manager. It is essential to estimate the costs involved and the resources needed to undertake the project, but this requires significant judgment to plan the overall workloads, allowing flexibility to accommodate the inevitable changes that will occur. Planning in too great a level of detail and using it to precisely schedule activities is a time-consuming process that is almost impossible to maintain. Therefore a pragmatic approach is needed that uses the resource plan as the baseline for tracking expenditure and assessing progress towards delivering the key milestones.

Several project management software packages have tools for creating a task matrix such as that shown in Table 8.3. This type

Table 8.3 *The task matrix*

Resource Matrix			Project Number 8543					
Stage no.	Activity	Total time	Person/ facility	Time required				
				Jan.	Feb.	Mar.	Apr.	Total
1	Concept design	70 days	J. Brown	6	3	10	13	32
			P. Smith	5	8	13	12	38
2	Concept model	30 days	P. Smith					
	↓		↓					
	↓		↓					
9	Evaluation		Test rig					

of document shows the allocation of resources and names people assigned to the various work packages. When planning resources, consideration should also be given to the loading on critical items of equipment that might be required by more than one project team. The planning units should be appropriate to the size and duration of the tasks – that is, hours, days, weeks, months – and the matrix should be used to determine the resources needed to complete the various tasks and the overall workload of people responsible for performing the tasks.

This information is crucial when the business is proposing to undertake several projects, since there is always a tendency to launch more projects that the company can adequately resource and individuals with specialist skills become totally overwhelmed. Therefore, this information enables best use of resources to be made by planning the workload around achievable schedules. When preparing the company business plan, collating the resources requirements and budgets needed to fund the development programme is an essential factor when determining which projects the company should invest in. The management team must decide on the balance between delivering operating profits and cash, and those projects that are critical for securing future prosperity. Expenditure on developing the business must be established on the basis of what the company can afford.

Once the resource requirement and time scales for the project have been established, they should be translated into a budget that collates all the costs associated with delivering the project objectives. This means product introduction projects require the manpower resources derived in the phased work packages to be translated into actual expenditure. This is achieved by establishing a charge rate that absorbs the overheads associated with employing engineers to work on the team, and is usually about two or three times the base salary costs. This, together with other project expenses, enables a revenue expenditure plan to be prepared. Capital expenditure needed for plant and equipment plus associated revenue expenses must also be identified separately using a similar time-phased plan to create a complete expenditure and cash-flow budget.

Typical cost categories include:

- Labour costs (both internal and external);
- All materials and charges;
- Cost of facilities not included in the labour overhead;

- Contingencies for changes to specification or unforeseen events;
- License costs for technology/consultants;
- Hardware and software maintenance charges
- Factory hardware needed prior to installation of production facility;
- Cost of spares and maintenance to support product field trials;
- Travel subsistence and miscellaneous expenses;
- Test equipment and facilities;
- Pre-production tooling and materials handling; and
- Entry fees.

A formal budget must be prepared for each significant project and then compiled at company level by the programme office to obtain an overall time-phased project expenditure plan. Estimates must also be prepared for the on-going development work needed to maintain products in current production. These must be submitted and taken into account when setting overall budgets in the business plan. A similar resource planning and budgeting process is required for change projects.

PROJECT CONTROL

The project manager is responsible for maintaining progress towards delivering the project objectives within budgeted expenditure limits. This is achieved by establishing review mechanisms that identify any deviations to the plan at the earliest possible time, and instigating corrective actions needed to recover the situation.

Project control is normally effected through a series of meetings, using standard agendas and attended by designated groups of people:

- *Daily review* with *project manager* – held in the project office for 15 minutes with the project team to record daily progress, identify problems and update action sheets.
- *Weekly meeting* with *project owner* – held in meeting room for one to two hours with the full project team to identify actions, review progress on actions, and provide guidance for resolving outstanding problems.
- *Monthly meetings* with *project owner*: held in conference room for one to two hours with the project team, programme director and appropriate senior managers to receive formal presentation, and provide feedback on progress.

- *Milestone review* with *senior management* – held with the general manager, programme director and other executive team members to confirm the direction, support the proposed action plan and release expenditure.

Each formal meeting should generate a set of actions, that are assigned an owner with an expected completion date appropriate to recovering or maintaining the project plan. These action sheets are an essential part of the project management process and provide an integrated checklist of items that must be accomplished to achieve the project objectives:

Action checklist						
No.	Date	Problem	Proposed action	Person responsible	Date required	Date achieved

A project manager controls the project to achieve the deliverables within cost targets and time milestones by:

- Controlling the level of resources assigned to complete work packages;
- Managing the activities required within the work package necessary to provide an acceptable solution;
- Establishing well-managed meetings and reporting structures to direct effort;
- Identifying potential risks at an early stage and taking action to resolve them;
- Selecting an appropriate team capable of delivering good quality work;
- Understanding and focusing upon the critical items that must be resolved;
- Creating a team environment with the commitment to succeed;
- Escalating problems that cannot be resolved by the project team within the organisation; and
- Seeking assistance within and outside the business to prevent duplication of effort.

The project manager's role on large projects requires similar skills to those of a general manager. Therefore, project management can be used a good developmental appointment for people with senior management potential.

PROJECT REPORTING

Progress reports providing an overview of events must become part of the monthly business management reporting system. Information for each project should be presented using a standard format summarising project and product costs and the achievement of project milestones.

Project Costs

These should be collected using a time-booking system for team members working on the project, with a cost-collection procedure that assigns the appropriate expenditures to the respective cost categories. These costs together with the capital expenditure elements should be formally reported as shown in Table 8.4. This information can be presented in tabular or graphical form provided it clearly shows the financial status of the project. The time and effort spent collecting these figures must reflect the financial risk being taken by the business but it is important not to burden the project with unnecessary administrative overhead tasks.

Product Cost

This cost is generally harder to determine because it depends upon estimated costs that are relatively difficult to calculate. Learner curves for predicting cost reductions that should be achieved through experience of manufacturing products and continuous improvement have also to be included. In most instances, a cost model will have been developed in order to obtain product and project approval, and commitments made based upon achieving these cost targets. Therefore this model should be used as the basis of the calculation, and the product cost refined as more accurate estimates of individual items

Table 8.4 *Project costs*

Project non-recurring costs

		Jan.	Feb.	Mar.	Apr.	May	Jun.	Jul.	Aug.
Actual expenditure	month								
Actual expenditure	cumul.								
Planned expenditure	month								
Planned expenditure	cumul.								
Under/(over) budget	month								
Under/(over) budget	cumul.								
Cost to completion									

Capital costs

		Jan.	Feb.	Mar.	Apr.	May	Jun.	Jul.	Aug.
Order commitments	month								
Order commitments	cumul.								
Actual payments	month								
Actual payments	cumul.								
Baseline plan	month								
Baseline plan	cumul.								
Actual under/(over) plan	month								
Actual under/(over) plan	cumul.								

become available. The cost of development parts are usually much greater than those manufactured on production equipment. Information should be presented tracking progress towards achieving the cost-base used to justify the business case. The level of detail and effort devoted to calculating the product cost should again depend upon the impact any deviation will have upon long-term business profitability.

Table 8.5 *Product costs*

Estimated product costs								
	Jan.	Feb.	Mar.	Apr.	May	Jun.	Jul.	Aug.
Actual product cost								
Latest estimated product cost								
Committed product cost								
Actual under/(over) committed								
Estimated under/(over) committed								

Achievement of Project Milestones

Tracking the progress towards delivering the work packages and key milestones should be routinely updated on the project plan by the project team. Software support packages are very useful for maintaining this type of information, but for management reporting chain charts provide a more visible method of tracking progress towards delivering the key milestones. The chart is constructed with equal time periods plotted on the horizontal and vertical axis with the origin being the start of the project. The sloping line (at 45 degrees) indicates when the milestones should be complete and links the corresponding dates. Each reporting period the project manager reviews the progress towards achieving all the key milestones in turn. If the milestone will be delivered on time then the line is drawn vertically for a one-month period. If the milestone has slipped the line is drawn to show the slippage that has occurred and similarly, if the project is ahead of schedule then the line shows the improvement in time scale that has occurred (Figure 8.4).

The chain chart provides an excellent visible summary of progress, making the project team consider the impact of slipping one due date upon the other project milestones. It also makes the project team act responsibly, because chains that start sloping in the month prior to the milestone being delivered cannot be repeated more than once if the project manager is to retain credibility.

244

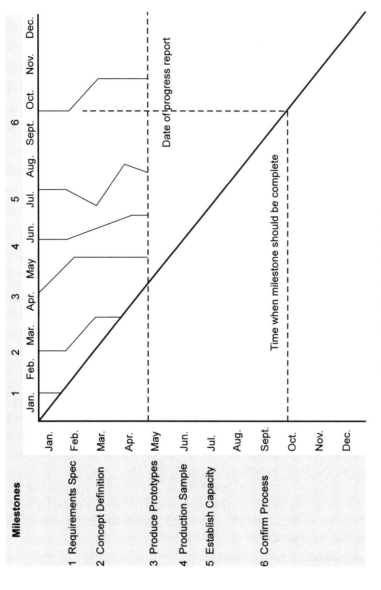

Figure 8.4 Typical chain chart

Project Manager's Comments

This should be a brief project report recording the month's achievements, any problems encountered and actions taken or proposed to achieve the milestones. The manager must also make a quantified assessment of the work to date, stating the quality and robustness of any deliverables

Adopting tailored standardised reporting procedures is essential when controlling a large number of projects. This can be readily accomplished using a good word-processing package, and circulating information using an electronic mail system. Once the project summary reports have been received into the programme office, the programme director's task is to generate an exception report for presentation to the business management team as a formal board report, highlighting achievements and areas of concern.

RISK MANAGEMENT

The early identification and management of risk is a primary project management task. It is the project manager's responsibility to ensure factual information is presented to the management team and that any possible 'surprises' are reported before they become a crisis. Risks are identified in several ways and everyone must participate in raising a concern and assessing the likely impact.

Risks in product introduction projects can occur due to changes in the following areas:

Commercial
- Market requirements impacting the planned capacity;
- Revised customers' requirements delaying the product launch;
- Product life-cycles creating modifications to specification;

Technical
- Completion dates revised to exploit a window of opportunity;
- New materials or processes failing to meet specification;
- Customers' requirements expanding the working envelope;

Business integrity
- Financial position under threat and additional cash needed to exploit the product;

- Legislation and legal standards that must be adopted for the product or process; and
- Availability of resources or technology needed for the programme.

This list only gives a few examples of where risks might arise. Risk assessment should be embodied within the project management process and become a routine procedure. It should be performed by a team of four or five people from different areas of the business before each major milestone review. The team should identify the possible risks, evaluating the impact each would have and the likelihood of it happening. The degree of risk can then be assessed by scoring various factors, and a list of alternative actions developed reflecting the likely impact upon the business and the customer. These considered proposals are then presented to the management review team, with actions needed to eliminate or minimise the risk formally agreed. Proposals dealing with high-category risks should adopt parallel solutions giving added security.

It should be noted that the *product* and *process* FMEA (failure mode and effect analysis) together with the *project classification* process provide a good initial assessment on the degree of risk posed by the project.

The other mechanism for identifying potential risks is through the formal reporting systems and *hazard* reports. These monthly reports provide information on performance against the financial budget, progress towards milestones and quality of deliverables. This information must be consistently scrutinised for deviations that could adversely impact the project if decisive corrective actions are not taken promptly.

HAZARD REPORTS

The *hazard* reporting procedure is a crucial element of an effective project management process. A *hazard* report is a mandatory form that must be raised and circulated across the organisation by the project manager or any member of the team, when the project deliverables are potentially at risk or *control parameters* fall outside the agreed limits. This simultaneously alerts the managing director, the programme office and all other senior managers associated with the project to a problem and possible corrective actions needed to recover the situation.

The *hazard* report should be a standard form that can be transmitted electronically directly onto the desk of senior managers, containing the following information:

- A full project reference, including the date raised plus a unique number that identifies the incident;
- Description of the hazard and the implication for the customer and company;
- Recovery options that are available and the impact these could have upon the business;
- List of recovery actions for that have already been taken to address the situation, with owners and committed delivery dates;
- Proposed action group listing the people assigned to work together and identify, agree and implement recovery plans/actions;
- Circulation list of people that must informed of the *hazard*; and
- Hazard closure statement that is completed once the situation has been recovered, or revised plans have been accepted by the management team and the customer.

Once a *hazard* report has been issued it is incumbent upon the project manager to ensure that regular progress reports, daily if necessary, are circulated until the problems have been fully resolved. The hazard is then closed by completing the last section of the standard form.

Control Parameters

Control parameters for a project should be agreed as part of the specification at the initiation of the project by the project owner and programme director. Measures used to trigger the system are dependent upon the business needs and the industry that is being served. However, they are usually associated with the following factors:

Cost
- Actual project expenditure has slipped against plan to a level of, say, 20 per cent;
- Cost to complete shows spend at the financial year's end will be overspent, say, 10 per cent;
- Project spend at the completion of the project will be overspent, say, 5 per cent;

Time
- Major internal project milestones outside acceptable limits and cannot be recovered, say, two months;
- Customer milestones are at risk, impacting the customer schedule, say, one month;
- Customer delivery dates are at risk, jeopardising the programme.

Quality of Deliverables
- The progress towards resolving technical problems is not being achieved;
- Product costs are outside those agreed in the project plan and initiatives to implement savings are not providing the expected reductions; and
- Customer genuinely concerned about the robustness of the programme.

The *hazard* reporting process provides an early warning system for issues that must be addressed by the senior management team. It also gives an open route for anyone in the project team to raise a concern that they feel is not being adequately addressed. It is important, therefore, that the managing director and programme director seriously consider every hazard report, taking a personal involvement in identifying the root cause of problems and instigating appropriate corrective actions.

CHANGE CONTROL

Throughout the project life-cycle, agreement is reached on many critical aspects that allow the project to progress through phase gates to the next stage. However, once a milestone has been achieved that confirms critical product or process parameters, a formal mechanism is needed to review and implement any proposed changes. All projects are subject to changes for a variety of reasons, therefore it is important to have a change control process that formally reviews and acknowledges the new requirements. The purpose of having a documented system is to:

- minimise the lead-time for implementing the change;
- inform everyone of the change, preventing expenditure on redundant schemes;
- track changes that have been requested;

- assess the impact in terms of time and cost;
- contain the number of requests ensuring they are authorised;
- ensure all documentation is amended to include the change; and
- formally accept the change and how it will be funded.

Product introduction projects that are being undertaken in collaboration with third parties are notorious for being subject to change requests, and unless these are routinely logged considerable financial loss can result.

The factors that trigger a change request come from a variety of sources but generally are a result of one or more of the following:

- Product does not meet specification on test;
- Customer needs to modify the specification requirements;
- Production cannot manufacture the component;
- New materials or processes not robust;
- Cost reduction;
- Failures in field trials or service;
- Errors in documentation, drawings, specification or clarification;
- Product enhancement to improve performance; and/or
- Recurring quality problems and non-conformance in production.

The method of handling change requests is by establishing a control mechanism based upon a change review board. This board is a multidisciplinary group of senior managers and engineers who meet on a regular basis, using a standard agenda to:

- Review and authorise all change requests;
- Confirm when a change has been accepted and will be implemented;
- Specify the information requirements and maintain recoverable documentation;
- Evaluate alternative solutions recommending the most cost-effective;
- Assess the impact of the change on the business;
- Agree the target dates and costs associated with implementation;
- Confirm who will pay for the change;
- Assign a manager to coordinate the activities and report progress;
- Prevent unnecessary change requests being adopted;
- Minimise disruption to the business; and
- Monitor the impact of change requests on customer satisfaction and financial performance of the business.

Establishing a change control procedure using standard documentation also provides the foundation of a factory quality system, by ensuring all changes to the product and process are documented and formally approved.

THE ROLE OF THE PROJECT MANAGER

The project manager is the key person for driving change and he or she is instrumental in planning, monitoring and controlling all aspects of the work, motivating team members to achieve high-quality project objectives on time and within agreed cost targets. The project manager integrates numerous complex activities needed to accomplish tasks and takes direct responsibility for managing the process. However he/she must have authority to take decisions within the parameters agreed by the management team and be given accountability for owning the expenditure budget with the flexibility to purchase resources from the most appropriate source. The level of activities may vary depending upon the type and size of project being undertaken but the skills required and personal commitment needed for delivering results remain consistent for all forms of project work.

The project manager:

- is project owner for delivering the project objectives, rigorously applying good-practice project management methods;
- is general manager for everyone working on the project team;
- is custodian of the programme and project management procedures;
- manages and controls day-to-day activities of team members;
- manages the project review process established to control and ensure management involvement;
- instigates a series of management reviews and meetings, taking responsibility for preparing action lists and implementing recommendations;
- is directly responsible for controlling the project and achieving customer, business and project objectives within the agreed time-scale and budget;
- coordinates formal agreements for the project specification and contractual terms required with the customer, government agencies and suppliers;

- agrees the technical performance specification with the appropriate managers for the product and process;
- maintains timely and accurate project documentation for project classification, project plans, expenditure and progress reports;
- conducts regular risk assessments using the project classification system, product FMEA and process FMEA taking action to limit the impact of possible changes to critical parameters;
- establishes methods for assessing the risk to achieving delivery promises, keeping expenditure within budget and maintaining the quality of deliverables;
- ensures the management team are not exposed to unplanned 'surprise' events;
- assesses the magnitude of problems, taking action to minimise the impact and recover any slippage;
- reports to the management in the manner required by the company;
- implements without compromise the technical standards, production methods and quality requirements as specified by the manager responsible;
- in conjunction with other managers, prepares the business case for obtaining project approval;
- establishes the project master plan and maintains a history file, including change requests;
- decides where to allocate the work packages based upon availability of resources, areas of expertise, cost, customer preference and preferred supplier agreements;
- secures wherever possible external grants to recover project expenditure;
- establishes a project management structure with the appropriate people and skills required to complete the range of project work packages;
- takes the final decision on team selection;
- identifies the training needed by team members;
- approves all expenditures within the authorised limits agreed by the management team in the *project summary*;
- coordinates activities of full and part-time team members, marketing, customer account managers, technical specialists, product designers, development engineers, manufacturing experts, purchasing and commercial resources, assigned to meet the project objectives;
- monitors and implements corrective actions;

- ensures that cost collection codes are used for expenditure on internal spend, outside purchases, travel, capital expenditure and tooling and so on;
- ensures all project costs are documented, reviewed and rigorously controlled;
- ensures people assigned full-time to the project team work on the project, except for specialists who undertake specific tasks;
- undertakes joint performance appraisals for team members in conjunction with departmental managers;
- ensures formal monthly project summary reports are forwarded to the programme office and when necessary the customer;
- raises and circulates hazard reports if project time-scales, development costs, product costs or quality of deliverables move outside the established hazard criteria limits; and
- reviews the release of confidential information and reports presented in the technical press, conferences and other publications.

The responsibilities and magnitude of tasks for major projects may be too large for a single project manager to manage effectively. Therefore a structure should be considered that assigns work packages to other project managers, creating a management organisation with project managers reporting to a programme manager who takes overall responsibility for delivering the objectives.

SUMMARY

Project management has been used for several years by companies working across a number of industries. In my experience, many very successful companies are good at project management: it provides the mechanism for implementing change and exploiting the power of the team over individual effort. The disciplines needed for effective project management require traditional functional activities to be replaced with multidisciplinary teams that are assembled to undertake a specific task. The nature of the project team changes depending on the demands of the work packages, and once complete the team is disbanded with people returning to a previous job or moving into another team. The project management support tools must be standardised and tailored to the requirements of the business, ensuring a correct balance is obtained providing formal informative reports and not non-value added paperwork.

The work involved preparing and updating project management information can be reduced by adopting suitable commercially available software packages, but judgment is still needed concerning the level of detail necessary to control the project and identify financial risks. Once fully implemented, project management becomes a normal way of working and teams are naturally formed to implement change across all areas of the business.

9

Finance Management

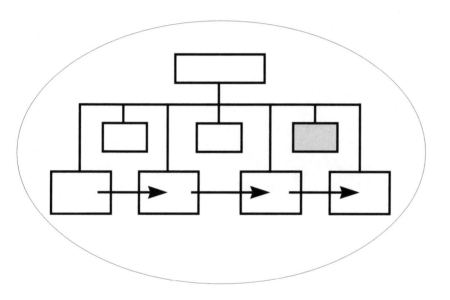

Topics

Introduction
Financial reporting
Forecasting results
Financial control
Costing systems
Non-financial measures of performance
Business awareness and understanding
Investment sanctions
Capital sanctions
Summary

9

Finance Management

INTRODUCTION

Financial management is the foundation of a good business. Companies must have robust financial control systems that ensure the commitments made to the managing director are delivered. The three most important elements are *profit, cash* and *return on capital employed,* and it is the responsibility of the finance director to exert financial controls to continually manage the business performance. Most finance departments are functionally orientated with similar divisions of labour to those found in other business activities. Therefore the finance team's area of responsibility must be expanded from the traditional role of producing legal accounts into a service department providing accurate and timely management information supporting the total business process.

This can only be achieved through introducing standardised reporting systems providing relevant information suitable for high-level consolidation, but with sufficient detail to be used for closer hands-on management. Information collected by the finance department should also to be restructured to include both financial and non-financial information, providing a sound basis for making decisions, and used across the organisation to control operational performance and give feedback to the workforce.

FINANCIAL REPORTING

The reporting of financial information must be accurate and timely. This should be achieved by establishing a standard set of figures that are collected at the end of each accounting period, normally monthly, and released within two days for management review. The earlier this financial information is available, the easier it is to take corrective actions to address the situation. The collection and preparation of information does not add value, so should be automated whenever possible to allow more time for analysing the results and determining actions necessary to drive business performance.

The financial information should be structured under three headings:

Performance in Month (or Accounting Period)
- *Actual* performance achieved and reported;
- *Budgeted* performance committed to the managing director in the business plan;
- *Forecast* representing the latest estimate that was accepted prior to start of accounting period;

Cumulative Performance in the Year to Date
- *Actual* performance achieved;
- *Budgeted* performance committed in the business plan;
- *Forecast* representing an estimate of the results, made after the plan was accepted;
- *Last year's* reported performance;

Year-end Targets Committed in the Business Plan
- *Budgeted* performance agreed and committed in the business plan;
- *Forecast* performance representing the best estimate at a specific date after the business plan was accepted; and
- *Last year's* reported result.

The reported information must be directly relevant to managing the business and presented in a summarised format that captures sufficient detail to identify specific causes of deviations against budgeted performance. The type of information that should be reported covers the following:

Sales
- Original equipment sales.
- Repair and overhaul sales.
- Service and replacement parts.
- Engineering services and contracts.
- Share of associated companies.
- Inter-trading with the company.
  - ⇒ Total sales

Profit
- Original equipment margin.
- Repair and overhaul margin.
- Service and replacement parts margin.
- Others.
  - ⇒ Factory margin

  Net
- Product introduction expenditure.
- Business development.
- Selling and distribution costs.
- Head-office charges.
- Provisions and duplicated profit from intertrading.
- Associated companies.
  - ⇒ Trading profit

- Major restructuring and change projects.
- Redundancy and closure costs.
- Other exceptional items.
  - ⇒ Profit before interest and tax

- Interest.
  - ⇒ Profit before tax

Cash Flow
- Profit before interest and tax.
- Plus depreciation charged against capitalised plant and equipment.
- Capital expenditure.
- Gross stocks.
- Payments on account.
- Operating debtors.
- Operating creditors.
- Other operating cash flow items.
  - ⇒ Operating cash flow

Balance Sheet
- Gross stocks.
- Debtors.
- Creditors.
- Progress payments on work carried out.
- Provisions investments.
- Fixed assets.
  - ⇒ Total capital employed

Business Ratios
- Stock to sales %.
- Stock turn on cost of sales.
- Return on capital employed.
- Return on sales.
- Capital turnover ratio.

Employees
- Full-time staff.
- Full-time hourly paid operatives.
- Part-time employees.
- Contract employees.
  - ⇒ Total employees

Employee Ratios
- Payroll costs.
- Sales/employee.
- Payroll/sales.
- Added value/employee.
- Added value/payroll costs.

Gross Margin Analysis
- Original equipment.
- Repair and overhaul.
- Service parts.

Additional, detailed cost information must also be collected and reported to underpin the operating performance, giving management knowledge of any adverse situations. The figures that should be presented, using a similar reporting structure, are:

Non-Payroll Overheads
- Depreciation.
- Rent, rates and local taxes.
- Gas, electricity, water, fuel oil.
- Consumable materials.
- Maintenance and repair of equipment.
- Insurance premiums.
- Operating leases on plant and equipment.
- Security.
- Others.
  - ⇒ Total facilities and equipment

- Customer development projects.
- Advertising and promotion.
- Distribution overheads.
- Freight, duty and packaging.
- External commissions.
- Bad debts.
- Others.
  ⇒ Total selling and distribution overheads

- Telephone, fax and communications.
- Travel and company cars.
- Entertaining and exhibitions.
- Professional fees and consultants.
- Others.
  ⇒ Total general overheads
  ⇒ Total non-payroll overheads

Product Introduction Costs
- Generic technology.
- New product development.
- Support of current products.
  ⇒ Net charge to profit in the period

Analysis of Gross Stocks
- Raw materials and bought-out parts.
- Work in progress.
- Maintenance and consumable items.
- Original equipment warehouse.
- Service stores.
  ⇒ Total gross stock

Analysis of Operating Debtors
  ⇒ Trade debtor days

Analysis of Operating Creditors
  ⇒ Trade creditor days

Analysis of Provisions

Order Book
- Order book for third-party sales.
- Orders received.
- Booked orders/billed orders.
- Current year gap of orders required to meet current year's sales plan.

This list is comprehensive and must be tailored to meet the specific business requirements. However, this level of detail is necessary to allow the management team to understand the issues and make appropriate informed decisions needed for effective hands-on management.

FORECASTING RESULTS

This difficult, imprecise task has to be routinely performed at the request of the managing director. The information is usually restricted to the top-line figures with predictions being made by synthesising the trend of sales, analysing detailed operational performance over the past months, making adjustments for changes that should occur due to actions already taken, and experience of past events. Accurate forecasting is critical for the senior management team as they prepare to talk to investors and release financial statements concerning the business results. The crucial requirement is to be *correct* because managing directors do not appreciate 'surprises', and, once a forecast has been accepted, over-achievement is practically as damaging as failing to deliver budget. The ability to provide accurate forecasts is a primary requirement for the finance director, as errors are often not forgiven.

FINANCIAL CONTROL

Financial control is critical for any business and the finance director must exert considerable authority to protect the company's financial performance on profit, cash and return on capital employed. Therefore it is important that any short-term measures that have to be imposed do not cause lasting damage to the business, customers or suppliers. At a company level, actions must be directed at areas causing problems, reinforcing the need for detailed information on:

- Number of employees working in different areas;
- Controllable non-payroll overheads;
- Product introduction expenditure;
- Stock analysis by product line;
- Customers failing to settle outstanding accounts;
- Suppliers that may extend credit; and
- List of provisions and reserves.

It is far more preferable to *plan* how savings will be made as part of the business planning process, than having to accept crash measures imposed to prevent a financial crisis. These panic measures often fail to rectify the situation and leaves an unnecessary legacy of damaged relationships.

Good financial control stems from an in-depth analysis of financial and non-financial information. Generally, finance departments must devote more time to understanding the information and interpreting the possible consequences of poor performance, so corrective action can be taken at an early stage before the situation is manifest as a major problem.

COSTING SYSTEMS

Costing systems in manufacturing companies are relatively complex and often based upon overhead absorption techniques for determining the cost of manufacturing components. Direct material and bought-out component costs can be readily determined, with allowances made for materials lost in process and the cost of direct labour adding value, but it is the overheads and indirect activities that are difficult to apportion. Traditionally, this has been achieved using overhead absorption to produce a factory index rate. This provides a multiplying factor to be applied to the hourly labour rate, giving the cost of producing the part. This system was devised for functional factories where the cost of, for example, the drilling section, the turning section or the milling section were in proportion to the time a person spent on the job. However, in today's industrial climate where machines perform most of the operations and possibly run unattended, using a system based upon a person's direct input totally distorts the cost model. This is manifest when used to compare the cost of different jobs. Those products that are manufactured on modern machines are totally underpriced compared to traditional running jobs still needing manual operations. This error is compounded when management use the information to assess product-line profitability and take the wrong decisions. It is important, therefore, that the costing systems are redesigned to reflect the actual costs associated with producing a range of components.

The restructuring of production facilities into modules that take responsibility for producing a range of similar products or components provides the opportunity to also redesign the costing system, reflecting actual activity costs associated with manufacturing particular product ranges. Care must be taken to prevent the cost system from becoming over-complex and too difficult to use for planning, monitoring and control purposes. This should be achieved by applying a subset of the information needed for *financial reporting* to determine a budget and control variable costs.

Costs that can be assessed and allocated to different modules across the factory include:

- Materials and bought-out components;
- All labour within the module, irrespective of direct or indirect work;
- Depreciation on equipment;
- Cost of tooling and fixtures;
- Space rental charge proportional to area occupied;
- Consumable materials;
- Fair allocation of gas, water, and fuel oil;
- Maintenance and repair of equipment;
- Operating leases on equipment;
- Cost of holding stock in the module;
- Cost of scrap and rectification;
- General overhead and supervision; and
- Other services used in the manufacturing process.

This produces a set of standards representing more accurately the cost of manufacture within each area. A rate can then be applied to machining times for components in a machining module, or the time a person spends assembling products in an assembly and test area. The other advantage of this technique is that it underpins the high-level reporting system, allowing informed management intervention.

NON-FINANCIAL MEASURES OF PERFORMANCE

Finance departments have traditionally been concerned with collecting only financial information, but this is not adequate for monitoring the overall business performance. Performance measures have been defined for *customer satisfaction* and *quality and supply-chain management*, and these need to be incorporated into the business reporting package. Collecting information must become an integral part of people's job roles, giving sufficient detail to provide a comparison of performance levels over time. Great care must be taken to prevent this recording of information from becoming a significant non-value-added task. All information must be relevant for managing operations, and have an owner that needs it.

The measures identified for monitoring must be specifically designed to drive key business issues and chosen with full knowledge that people will deliver what is measured, without necessarily considering the consequences. Non-financial parameters and ratios that may be considered important for production operations include the following:

Labour/Capacity
- Working days in the month.
- Number of hours available for work in month.
- Total attendance hours.
- Operational attendance hours.
- Overtime hours worked by operators.
- Lost hours through absenteeism and sickness.
- % overtime/attendance hours.
- % absenteeism/attendance hours.
- Time spent training.
- Number of industrial accidents and environmental incidents.

Productivity
- Number of employees assigned to each module.
- Number employed in supervision and general support.
- Number of units produced per person.
- Number of units produced per unit of floor space.
- Sales value per unit of floor space.
- Sales per employee.
- Added value per employee.
- Added value per unit of pay.
- Total number of standard hours produced in period.
- Standard hour per person.
- Efficiency = standard hours produced/attendance hours.
- % cost bought-out items/sales.
- % cost direct labour/sales.
- % cost factory support/sales.
- % cost overheads/sales.

Machine Capacity/Capability
- Number of key machines.
- % utilisation = actual time machine manned/available hours.

- % planned down time/available hours.
- Unplanned downtime in period.
- % unplanned downtime/available hours.
- Number of machines checked for process capability in month.
- % key machines verified as capable.
- Number of measuring systems checked for capability in month.
- % of measuring systems verified as capable.
- % of processes controlled using statistical methods.
- % accuracy of data on the production control database.

Stock
- Stock turns.
- % stock in raw material.
- % bought-out components.
- % work in progress.
- % finished goods.
- % service parts and repairs.

Schedule Adherence
- Value of sales loaded on master production schedule/budgeted sales.
- % of master production schedule delivered in first 20% of period.
- % of master production schedule delivered in 40% of period.
- % of master production schedule delivered in 60% of period.
- % of master production schedule delivered in 80% of period.
- % total achievement of master production schedule.
- % achievement of original equipment deliveries to customer's requirement date.
- % achievement of spares sent to customer's request date.

Supplier Performance
- % of items delivered on time to master production schedule.
- % of items rejected for inferior quality.
- Number of changes made to customer schedules.

Lead-times
- Average lead-time on the production control system for in-house manufacture.
- Average lead-time on the production control system for bought-out items.
- Actual lead-time for main product lines.
- Actual lead time for service parts.
- Actual lead-time for bought-out items/materials.

Quality
- Cost of quality-assurance activity.
- Cost of internal failure – rework, scrap and rectification.
- cost of external failure – returns, recalls and modifications.
- % cost of quality-assurance activities/sales.
- % cost of internal failure/sales.
- % cost of external failure/sales.
- % of products rejected first time at assembly and test.
- Equipment returns/dispatches.
- Product conformance, number of concessions granted to production.

The most difficult factor to measure, particularly in low-volume, high-variety component manufacturing facilities, is labour productivity. This can be accomplished for comparison purposes by collecting the number of standard hours produced over the period, but with the drive to reduce work content and associated standard hours through continuous improvement and self-managed work groups, any changes may have an adverse affect upon traditional productivity measures.

An appropriate set of non-financial measures are fundamental for managing the business, and extremely powerful when used in conjunction with the financial information. The range of measures outlined focuses upon operational aspects of the business which normally have established work measurement procedures. Consideration should also be given to developing similar relevant *measures of performance* for the other business processes, ensuring they also contribute to delivering a continual improvement in business performance. However, it is important to establish standard definitions and reporting formats for all the proposed measures. This makes sure everyone uses the same factors when performing the calculations, allowing accurate interpretation and cross-company comparisons to be made.

BUSINESS AWARENESS AND UNDERSTANDING

The finance function is the custodian of business information. Therefore it is incumbent upon it to collate critical aspects of operational performance and to inform the workforce about the state of the company. Employees need to be made aware of the company's

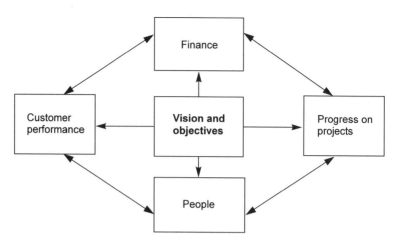

Figure 9.1   Balanced scorecard

trading position, and the progress being made toward achieving
business goals. This information should be presented as a balanced
scorecard such as that shown in Figure 9.1.

The information required for presentation, using a standard format tailored to specific areas of the company, should provide a
summary of the vision and strategy with defined objectives and
targets:

Customer Performance
- Customer measures based on quality, delivery and price.
- Customer perception monitor with comments from major custo-
  mers.
- Delivery to schedule by product line.
- Rejects received from the customer and corrective actions taken.
- Quality impact upon profit.

Financial Performance
- Sales of original equipment.
- Sales of service items.
- Profitability and trading prospects of business.
- Stock performance.
- Order book.
- Specific key measures of performance for the module or process
  area (supply chain – measures of performance).

Progress on Projects
- Summary and outline plan of projects that will affect the area.
- Achievements to date and problems to be resolved.
- Significant new product introduction projects and customer orders.
- Competitor activities.
- Key customer requirements for selecting suppliers.
- Investments in new plant and equipment.
- New information technology initiatives.

People
- Improvements in operational performance through continuous improvement groups.
- Impact of time lost through absenteeism.
- Training requirement and skills matrix.
- Job opportunities to work in other areas and expand range of skills and experience.
- Recognition of employees that have performed beyond expectation.
- Social activities and events.

The information presented must be relevant to the people receiving it, focusing upon issues that are important to them. The more feedback that is given, the greater effort people usually make to ensure the company is successful, and in return gain increased job satisfaction and security of employment. One way to successfully provide this information feedback is on designated display boards that are readily accessible to employees but can be screened if necessary for security purposes. All information displayed must be regularly updated and used as a focal point for regular group meetings to discuss issues facing the business, identifying ways of improving customer satisfaction and business performance.

INVESTMENT SANCTIONS

All progressive businesses must invest in change programmes involving expenditure on capital plant and equipment, and the finance director has the responsibility of providing the funds to finance these proposals. Therefore, the company needs a sanctioning procedure for all amounts over an agreed expenditure limit. This allows senior managers and directors to understand the overall requirements and formally sign to accept the expenditure being made on the specific items of new plant and equipment identified in the investment sanction. The business plan should have identified the main expenditure requirements throughout the planning period, and these will have been developed in greater detail as an integral part of a product introduction or change project. However, before money can be committed on major items of capital equipment, the finance director must insist on the expenditure being authorised and in return ensure funds are available to pay for it.

The company should have an established procedure for sanctioning significant capital investment. The type of information that should be provided using standard formats at this initial stage is:

Summary
- Name of business requesting the sanction.
- Outline of the proposal and the reasons why the expenditure is necessary.
- Cost involved for capital equipment and associated revenue expenditure.
- Date when the cash will be committed and the time scale for the expenditure.

Proposition for Investment
- Introduction and the business position.
- Market background and business opportunity that makes the investment case.
- Business plan and how the proposed expenditure relates to the business strategy.
- Performance improvement targets and financial commitments that are made possible through the investment.
- Personnel issues that need to be addressed, including skills shortages and training requirements.
- Financial appraisal and justification including cash-flow statements and break-even analysis.
- Risk analysis and further potential opportunities not included in the justification.
- Impact upon shareholder value and earnings per share.
- Top-line project plan with key milestones.
- Conclusion and recommendations.

Investment Plan
- Aims and deliverables from the investment.
- Approach taken identifying and selecting appropriate methods and technologies, with an analysis of the strengths and weaknesses of the alternative solutions.
- Description of the business operation area that will benefit from the investment.
- Item of equipment to be purchased.
- A short-list of suitable suppliers.
- Maximum capital cost including tooling, fixtures and additional items to make the process capable.
- Revenue expenditure needed to support the installation.
- Cost of training and suitable providers.
- Latest order date for delivery to meet project schedule.
- Delivery date required.
- Options on payment terms and conditions of purchase.

Rationale for Equipment Selection
- Current method and procedures for operations involved.
- Options available, analysing the concepts, strengths and weaknesses.
- Recommended preferred option and reasons for selection.
- Outline machine specification and key functional requirements.
- Operating tolerances compared to product definition and specification.
- Maximum total package cost.
- Delivery lead-time required by suppliers.

Formal Sanction Approval
- Brief project summary on single sheet, signed by the managers supporting the expenditure.
- Authorising signatures of the managing director, finance director, general manager and programme director.

This information is usually formally presented to the senior management team, followed by discussion allowing them to question and review the overall business case. Once the full ramifications for the company have been considered, if acceptable the proposal is signed giving the authority for the project to proceed. This triggers the detailed work of establishing the full specification, identifying the preferred supplier and raising capital sanctions against which the equipment may be purchased.

CAPITAL SANCTIONS

Once the investment sanction has received management approval, the next stage is to prepare the capital sanctions for each significant item of capital equipment. This is the formal documentation signed by the senior management team, giving authority to raise a purchase order for the new plant and equipment. The sanction documentation should be structured to request all relevant technical and supporting information for those factors that need to be addressed, prior to signing a purchase order with a supplier. The list should be tailored to satisfy the business needs, considering the following aspects:

Technical Specification, Requirements and Associated Estimated Costs
- Detailed machine specification.
- Special options and auxiliary equipment.
- Tooling and fixtures.
- Material handling facilities and pallets.
- Storage for tooling and pallets.
- Programming of parts needed for commissioning.
- Re-engineering and tooling for existing components.
- Foundations and environmental requirements.
- Power supply, cooling system and other services.
- Switch gear and electrical connections.
- Control systems, computers and communications.
- Software, translators and post processors.
- Interfaces to existing equipment.
- Agreed performance criteria for acceptance, including capability guarantees.
- Integration of equipment into existing systems.
- Warranty agreements and expected service life.
- Service contracts and time intervals between servicing.
- Service items to be purchased, including chemical substances.
- Penalties for late delivery or failing to meet performance criteria.
- Negotiated cost of total package.
- Agreed delivery date.
- List of equipment being replaced.
- Current book value of equipment and tooling being replaced.
- Allowances and trade-in value of existing equipment.
- Costs associated with removal and disposal of old equipment.

- Payment options available from the supplier, and leasing alternatives.
- Preferred terms and conditions of payment.

Additional Items that should be Addressed
- Control and disposal of waste materials and chemicals.
- Health and safety requirements for operating the process.
- Noise levels and acoustic screening requirements.
- Conformance to international standard for machine safety.
- Responsibility for installation of equipment.
- Removal and future use or disposal of existing equipment.
- Area of factory space released or required.
- Responsibility for machine-commissioning and associated costs.
- Running times and proposed utilisation of equipment.
- Agreed change-over times.
- Measuring systems to be used in production.
- Process capability of measuring system and critical parameters of components.
- Routine maintenance requirements.
- Proposed preventative maintenance schedule and responsibilities.
- Packaging and freight costs.
- Removal of packaging and materials used for commissioning.
- Preparation and refurbishment of facilities.

Revenue Expenditure to Support the Investment
- Training needed to operate the equipment.
- Material required for training and trials.
- Relocation of existing plant and equipment.
- Closure and reinstating buildings.
- Disposal of existing liabilities.
- Environmental and ground surveys to confirm the site is not contaminated.
- Preparation of operating procedures and quality systems.
- Training in quality procedures.
- Obtaining third-party quality approval for products and processes.
- Licenses to operate the equipment.
- Upgrades to keep the equipment current with latest standard.
- Cleaning procedures and disposal of effluents.
- Service contracts and agreements.

Expenditure Request
- Summary of the performance specification.
- Special options and auxiliary items of equipment.
- List of factors that must be addressed as part of the investment.
- Formal quotation giving the price of the capital items of equipment.
- Cost of addressing the other factors.
- Revenue expenditure required to support the investment.
- Cash-flow statement.
  ⇒ Total expenditure request

Savings and Returns
- Saving to be secured by the investment.
- Pay-back period in months.
- Date of order commitment.
- Date of payment.
- Discounted cash-flow statement for the investment.
- Sale price of existing equipment.

The information required needs to be relevant to the business and appropriate to the type of equipment being purchased. By introducing a discipline to consider operational requirements, all items of expenditure must be considered prior to placing the order. This can avoid the embarrassing situation of having to raise supplementary sanctions for additional expenditure to complete the job. The capital sanction should be raised and completed by the managers that require the investment, supported by the general manager of the site and subsequently authorised by the finance director, programme director, purchasing manager and the managing director. However, the system must be organised to authorise capital sanctions within a few days of the request being made for those projects based upon an approved business plan and investment sanction.

SUMMARY

The finance activity has a major influence on company performance, but its traditional focus upon financial accounts must be expanded into becoming the custodian of business information. The collated information must be relevant and accurate because it is fundamental for managing the business. It must also be timely to allow informed judgments, improving the quality of management decision-making. The finance team have the responsibility for selecting the key parameters that must be controlled to deliver the financial performance committed in the business plan. General managers survive by delivering those items that get measured, and consequently it is incumbent upon the finance activity to ensure the critical parameters needed to drive the short and long-term interests of the business are accurately defined and controlled. The sanctioning process for capital expenditure must be rigorous but also responsive to the business needs, and the routine of delaying sanctions and payments to suppliers for short-term cash objectives must be replaced by good financial planning and control.

Conclusion

This book has attempted to provide the framework for preparing a robust business plan structured around the fundamental business processes. The core processes together with the staff support activities have been broadly defined, providing a template for managers facing the challenge of implementing more effective business processes. All companies have different requirements depending upon the industry sector and the structure of business, but the generic processes have been defined as:

- Business Development and Sales
- Product Introduction Management
- Supply-chain Management
- Distribution and Aftermarket Support

In larger or more complex organisations these core processes are supported by three staff activities that operate in a matrix mode across the business. These roles are:

- Customer Satisfaction and Quality
- Programme Management
- Finance

These core processes and support activities have to be designed to meet specific business requirements and evaluated critically prior to implementation, but it is the introduction of effective business processes that provides the step change in business performance needed to be competitive in global markets. The transition inevitably creates uncertainties requiring skilful management; people must accept increased team responsibility linked to new ways of working. However, once implemented and supported by a commitment to continuous improvement, the transformation in all aspects of a business are incredibly rewarding. People working together in teams establish new levels of confidence, developing a motivation to win both for the company and themselves. This leads to business growth through reducing overall costs and delighting customers.

References and Supporting Literature

Allen, D. (1993) *Developing Successful New Products* (London: *Financial Times* and Pitman Publishing).

Bhote, K. R. (1988) *World Class Quality* (Cambridge, Mass.: American Management Association, Productivity Press).

Clark, K. B. and Wheelwright, S. C. (1995) *Leading Product Development* (Cambridge, Mass.: Harvard Business School Press).

Clarke, L. (1994) *The Essence of Change* (Englewood Cliffs, N.J.: Prentice-Hall).

Cooper, R. (1993) *Winning at New Products* (Reading, Mass.: Addison-Wesley).

Drew, S. (1994) 'BPR in Financial Services: Factors for Success', *Long Range Planning*, vol. 27, no. 5.

Hammer, M. and Champy, J. (1993) *Reengineering the Corporation* (London: Nicholas Brealey).

Hill, T. (1985) *Manufacturing Strategy* (London: Macmillan).

Japan Management Association (1989) *Kanban and Just in Time at Toyota; Management Begins at the Workplace*, trans. D. Lu (Cambridge, Mass.: Productivity Press).

Kennedy, C. (1994) 'Reengineering the Human Costs and Benefits', *Long Range Planning*, vol. 27, no. 5.

Lucas Engineering and Systems (1995) *Mini Guides*, CSC, Dog Kennel Lane, Solihull, England.

Parnaby, J. (1985) 'A Systems Approach to the Implementation of JIT Methodologies in Lucas Industries', *International Journal of Productivity Research*, vol. 26, no. 3.

—— (1991) 'Designing Effective Organisations', *International Journal of Technology Management*, vol. 6.

—— (1994) 'Business Process Systems Engineering', *International Journal of Technology Management*, vol. 9.

—— (1995) 'Design of the New Product Introduction Process to achieve World-Class Benchmarks', *IEE Proceedings on Science Measurement and Technology*, vol. 5.

Perigord, M. (1990) *Achieving Total Quality Management* (Cambridge, Mass.: Productivity Press).

Peters, T. (1990) 'Get Innovative or Get Dead', *California Management Review*, vol. 33, no. 1.

Rackham, N. (1987) *Making Major Sales* (Hampshire: Gower).

Time Management International (1992) *Putting People First*, TMI, Henley in Arden, Warwickshire, England.

Turner, F. (1993) 'Business Systems Engineering', *Proceedings of the Institute of Mechanical Engineers*, vol. 208.

Walsh, C. (1993) *Key Management Ratios* (London: *Financial Times* and Pitman Publishing).

Womack, P. J. and Jones, D. T. and Roos, D. (1990) *The Machine that Changed the World* (London: Maxwell Macmillan International).

Womack, P. J. and Jones, D. T. (1994) 'From Lean Production to Lean Enterprise', *Harvard Business Review*, March–April.

Young, T. L. (1994) *Leading Projects: a Manager's Pocket Guide* (London: The Industrial Society).

Index

account attractiveness 188–9
account classification 188–9
account strategy 190–1
acquisitions 55
action log 218
action sheets 240
added-value content 177, 178, 179
aftermarket *see* distribution and
aftermarket
alliances 55
appraisal
business appraisal 113–14, 116,
120–1, 127, 132
investment appraisal
review 123–5
sales-force appraisal 194–5
technical appraisal 114, 117–18,
121–2, 127–30, 133–4
approval
investment 123–5, 271
product 75–84
project 75–84, 235
assembly and test activities 149,
150–1
attractiveness
account 188–9
market 182–3, 184–5
audit of quality procedures 216

balance sheet 259
balanced scorecard 268–9
bid
draft bid proposal 83–4
preparation 84–9
submission of 90–2
bid approval review 88–9
branch positioning 184–6
brand 176

break-even analysis 172, 196
budgeting 238–9
business appraisal 113–14, 116,
120–1, 127, 132
business assessment: project
classification 87–9
business case: preparation of 82–4
business development and
sales 4–5
business plan 25–31
see also customer development
process
business ethics committee 207
business information
business intelligence
system 63–5
finance management and 267–9
business integrity 245–6
business objectives: summary
of 24–5, 58
business plan 21–58, 230, 238
customer satisfaction and
quality 47–9
distribution and
aftermarket 44–6
financial management and
control 50–5
introduction 23–5
product introduction 32–6
project management 49–50, 51
summary of business
objectives 24–5
supply-chain
management 36–44
business processes 3–4
generic 4, 4–5, 276
integrated *see* integrated
business processes
business ratios 52–3, 260

business strategy
  business plan 55–8
  development 11–15, 55–6
business support 5, 46–7, 276
buying factors, key 174–6, 190

capability: machine 217, 223,
    265–6
capacity 39
  internal factory capacity 150–5
  labour 265
  machine 265–6
capital expenditure 54, 233, 234
capital investors 228
capital sanctions 272–4
cash flow statement 54, 259
cellular organisation structures 43
  see also manufacturing modules/
    cells
chain charts 243–4
change
  configuration and change
    management systems 17
  process 227–30
  see also project management
change control process 124,
    248–50
change review board 249
changeover times reduction 43
chart-room 206–7, 232
coaching 193
code of ethical conduct 207–8
commercial changes 245
commercial compliance 223
commercial contract 125
commercial and financial
    planning 19
commercial investment appraisal
    review 123–5
commercial and market
    evaluation 81–2
commercial and technical reviews
  see review mechanisms

communication 10
  information technology 20
company ethics officer 208
competitive analysis 172, 182–6
competitive conditions 68
competitor profiles 31, 182
components: core 39, 41
computer-aided design
    (CAD) 17–18
computer-based process capability
    systems 218
concept validation 105, 106,
    118–23
  product release review 120–3
  tools and techniques 120
configuration and change
    management systems 17
continuous improvement 43, 130
contracts
  employment contracts 155
  formal commercial contract 125
  negotiation 90–2
control
  change control process 124,
    248–50
  financial control 262–3
  manufacturing control
    systems 18–19, 43, 156, 157
  project control 239–41
control parameters 246, 247–8
control systems 194
core components 39, 41
core technologies 32, 100
costing systems 263–4
costs 145
  associated with quality 48, 222
  bid preparation 86
  capital sanctions 272–3
  control parameters 247
  expectations 68
  financial reporting 260–1
  product costs 241–3
  product introduction 102–4, 261

project costs   233, 234, 237–9,
     241, 242
technical and cost
     evaluation   78–80
Cpk   217
creditors: analysis of   261
customer 'champions'   76
customer classification   187–8
customer development
     process   59–93
  bid preparation   84–9
  business intelligence
       system   63–5
  evaluation of
       requirements   69–75
  identification of
       opportunity   66–9
  ISO 9000 standard   215
  market forecast   62–3
  market overview   61–2
  opportunity evaluation
       process   65–92
  product and project
       approval   75–84
  winning the contract   90–2
customer-focused
     programmes   208–11
customer perception   48, 202–3,
     222
customer profiling   187
customer rating systems   201–2,
     222
customer satisfaction and
     quality   199–224
  business plan   47–9
  code of ethical conduct   207–8
  creating and communicating the
       vision   204–7
  establishing customer monitors
       and reporting
       systems   201–3
  formal quality
       procedures   214–16

IT systems   19
  performance measures   47–9,
       201–3, 222–3, 224
  quality-improvement
       process   211–13
  quality-improvement route
       maps   219–21
  safety review board   213–14
  statistical methods and process
       control   216–18
customer satisfaction and quality
     manager   5, 11
customer satisfaction route
     map   204, 205
customer schedule   75
customer segments   174–6, 190,
     191
  see also market segments
customer service systems   19
customer-specific price matrix   190
customers   228
  analysis of characteristics   29–31
  marketing and customer
       database   16–17
  performance information   268
  project classification and   74
  selection   187–8
  technical appraisal   127–8, 133
  trends and forecasting   176–9

debtors: analysis of   54, 261
delivery performance   48, 202, 223
demand-driven material flow
     systems   43, 156
demand expectations   68
design
  product   223
  product and process design   105,
       106, 111–18
design for assembly (DFA)   109–10
design of experiments
     (DOE)   110–11

design release   128
distribution and aftermarket   4, 5
  business plan   44–6
distribution management   169–97
  competitor profile   182
  customer selection   187–8
  customer trends and
      forecasting   176–9
  evaluation and appraisal   194–5
  key buying factors by market
      segment   174–6
  market attractiveness   182–3
  market flowout   172–4
  performance measures   46,
      195–6
  positioning the branch   184–6
  sales action processes   190–1
  sales-force effectiveness   193
  sales planning   188–90
  selling techniques   191–2
  strategic analysis   171–2
  strategic local market
      planning   180–1
  SWOT analysis   183
  tactical sales techniques   186
distribution overheads   261
distribution sales forecast   176–7,
    178, 179
divestments   55
documentation   43, 134
  change control   248–9, 250
  ISO 9000 standard   216
draft bid proposal   83–4

economic analysis   172, 196
electronic mail   20
employee development route
    map   9
employee ratios   260
employees   6–11, 228, 260
  communication   10
  development   10–11, 162
  finance management   268, 269
  IT personnel systems   19

supply-chain
    management   162–5
  working environment
      framework   9–10
employment contracts   155
engineering change control
      procedure   124
equipment   203
  capital sanctions   272–4
  investment sanctions   269–71
  overheads   260
  rationale for selection   271
  supply-chain
      management   145–8
ethical conduct: code of   207–8
evaluation
  commercial and market   81–2
  of customer requirements   69–75
  distribution management   194–5
  technical and cost   78–80
expenditure
  analysis of   44
  capital   54, 233, 234
  request   274
  to support capital
      investment   273

facilities and equipment
    overheads   260
factories   39, 40
  internal factory capacity   150–5
  space and location   141–5
factory margin   259
failure mode and effects analysis
    (FMEA)   110, 246
finance management   255–75
  business awareness and
      understanding   267–9
  business plan   50–5
  capital sanctions   272–4
  costing systems   263–4
  forecasting results   262
  investment sanctions   269–71

non-financial measures of
  performance   58, 264–7
finance manager   5
financial and commercial
  planning   19
financial control   262–3
financial performance   55, 268
  against previous business
    plan   53
  reporting   258
financial plan: for a project   234
financial ratios   52–3, 260
financial reporting   257–62
financial summary   52
fitting analysis   110
forecasting
  market forecast   62–3, 176–9
  results   262
functional analysis   109

government policies   81
gross margin   182–3, 184, 187, 190
gross margin analysis   260

handling analysis   109
hazard reports   50, 246–8
  control parameters   247–8
human resources   *see* employees

improvement teams   127, 210
industrial distribution
    management   *see* distribution
    management
industry trends   29
information   *see* business
    information
information technology   15–20, 43,
    65
  business plan   57–8
  networks and
    communications   20
integrated business processes   1–20
  business processes   3–4
  information technology   15–20

organisation structure   4–6
  people   6–11
  strategy development   11–15
integrity, business   245–6
Internet   20
inventory control   156
investment
  approval   123–5, 271
  proposition for   270
  requirements   69
investment plan   271
investment sanctions   269–71
ISO 9000 standard   161, 214–16
  requirements   214–16
isoplots   218

Japanese manufacturing
    philosophy   3
job 1   123, 127
just-in-time system   156

key buying factors   174–6, 190
key values   206–7

labour
  capacity   265
  productivity   265, 267
lead-times   266
leadership values   206–7
likelihood of success   184–5, 188–9
local market planning   180–1
location
  factory space and
    location   141–5
  site-location strategy   39, 40

machine capability   217, 223,
    265–6
machine capacity   265–6
machine inspection report   217
machining facilities   149–50, 152–4
'make vs buy' analysis   43, 140–1
management development   57
management structure   4–6

manufacturing
  conformance 129
  flow 41, 42
  system and equipment 145–8
  technical appraisal of
      process 117, 121–2
  technical appraisal of
      quality 133
manufacturing control
  systems 18–19, 43, 156, 157
manufacturing modules/cells 41,
  42, 127, 146, 263–4
manufacturing process
  definition 128–9
manufacturing support 105, 106,
  130–4
  sign-off review 132–4
  tools and techniques 131
manufacturing system
  engineers 168
manufacturing systems
  design 166–8
market analysis 172, 172–81
market attractiveness 182–3,
  184–5
market and commercial
  evaluation 81–2
market flowout 172–4
market forecast 62–3, 176–9
market overview 25–6, 61–2
market planning, local 180–1
market segments 26, 181
  key buying factors 174–6, 190,
    191
  sales by 176, 177, 178
market share: current and
  projected 26–8
marketing 182
  approach/options 80–1
  information 25–9
marketing and customer
  database 16–17
master production schedule 43,
  156

materials flow systems 43, 156
matrix pricing 190
measurement capability 218, 223
measures of performance
  (MoP) *see* performance
  measures
meetings: project control 239–40
  see also review mechanisms
milestones, project 100, 235, 243–4

networks 20
new product introduction *see*
  product introduction process
non-payroll overheads 260–1

objectives: business 24–5, 58
operating arrangements 151–5
opportunities
  evaluation 65–92
  identification 66–9
  SWOT analysis 55, 183
order book 261
organisation principles 57
organisation structure 4–6, 7, 43,
  56–7
original equipment manufacturers
  (OEM) 174, 175
overhead absorption 263
overheads: non-payroll 260–1

pay back 233
PC-based word processing,
  spreadsheet and presentation
  packages 20
people *see* employees
performance
  customer 268
  financial *see* financial
    performance
performance measures
  customer satisfaction and
    quality 47–9, 201–3, 222–3,
    224

distribution management   46,
   195–6
non-financial and finance
   management   58, 264–7
supply-chain
   management   156–9
personnel   *see* employees
PIRBIC system   192
politics: influence of   81
position   55
positioning the branch   184–6
pre-control charts   217, 218
price
   customer rating systems   202
   sensitivity   190
pricing   68–9, 86
   matrix   190
principles: organisation   57
process-based organisation   56–7
process capability   43, 217–18,
   223
   of measuring systems   218
process control   216–18
process design   105, 106, 111–18
process implementation   105, 106,
   123–30
   investment approval   123–6
   project launch review   127–30
   tools and techniques   126–7
process technology   74
product approval   75–84
product assessment square   184–5
product business plan   82–3, 124–5
product conformance   222
product cost   241–3
product data integrity   222
product data management
   systems   17
product definition   86
product design   105, 106, 111–18,
   222
product group market growth   29
product introduction costs   102–4,
   261

product introduction manager   5,
   11
product introduction plan   34, 35,
   100–1
product introduction process   4,
   95–136
   business plan   32–6
   concept validation   105, 106,
      118–23
   current project status   36, 38
   generic product introduction
      process   105–11
   identification of core
      technologies   32
   ISO 9000 standard   215
   manufacturing support   105,
      106, 130–4
   and opportunity evaluation   65
   process implementation   105,
      106, 123–30
   project classification   104–5
   project management   114, 118,
      122–3, 130, 134, 134–5
   resources   102–4
   simultaneous engineering   107
   supply-chain management   166,
      167
   team working   107–8
   technical resources   36, 37
   technology route map   32–4,
      97–100
   tools and techniques   108–11,
      116, 120, 126–7, 131
product launch review   127–30
product plan   34, 35, 100–1
product and process design   105,
   106, 111–18
   product and process design
      review   116–18
   proposal acceptance
      review   111–14
   tools and techniques   116
product quality   222
product release review   120–3

product segments 181
  sales by 176, 177, 178
  see also market segments
product service information 48
product technology 74
production
  capability 133
  confidence 129–30, 133–4
  state of readiness 129–30
production planning and
    control 18–19, 43, 156, 157
productivity: labour 265, 267
profit 222, 259
  sales and profit variance
      analysis 53–4
profitability 69
programme director *see* project
    manager
progress on projects 268, 269
project approval 75–84, 235
project classification 87, 104–5,
    246
  business assessment 87–9
  risk assessment 72–5
project control 239–41
project costs 233, 234, 237–9, 241,
    242
project management 225–53
  business plan 49–50, 51
  change control 248–50
  change process 227–30
  formal procedures 232–7
  hazard reports 246–8
  IT packages 16
  process 230–2
  product introduction
      process 114, 118, 122–3,
      130, 134, 134–5
  resource-planning and cost-
      estimating 237–9
  risk management 245–6
project manager 5, 97, 227
  control of project 240–1

product and project
    approval 76–8
  report 245
  role of 135, 250–2
project milestones 100, 235, 243–4
project plan 82, 235–7
project planning and
    preparation 78
project reporting 50, 241–5
  achievement of project
      milestones 243–4
  product cost 241–3
  project costs 241, 242
  project manager's
      comments 245
project schedule 74
project sign-off review 131–4
project status: current 36, 38
project summaries 34, 233, 235
project summary chart 50, 51
project summary report 134
project team 78, 252
  product introduction 130–1, 134
  team working 107–8
projected trends 26, 28
proposal acceptance
    review 111–14
purchasing 44

quality
  costs 48, 222
  customer rating systems 202
  customer satisfaction and
      quality *see* customer
      satisfaction and quality
  of deliverables 248
  manufacturing 133
  non-financial performance
      measure 267
quality function deployment
    (QFD) 108–9
quality-improvement
    process 211–13

quality-improvement projects 221
quality-improvement route
    maps 219–21
quality procedures 214–16
quality systems 161, 162–3

Rackham, Neil 192
ratios, financial 52–3, 260
red team/blue team reviews 76, 84
repeatability and reproducibility
    (R&R) studies 218
repeaters 41, 43
reporting
    financial 257–62
    hazard reports 50, 246–8
    project 50, 241–5
requirements
    evaluation of 69–75
    technical and capital
        sanctions 272–3
re-sellers 174, 175
resources
    planning 237–9
    product introduction
        resources 102–4
    technical 36, 37
returns 274
revenue expenditure 273
review mechanisms 105
    bid approval review 88–9
    evaluation of requirements 70–2
    investment appraisal
        review 123–5
    product launch review 127–30
    product and process design
        review 116–18
    product release review 120–3
    project control 239–40
    proposal acceptance
        review 111–14
    sign-off review 131–4
risk assessment 72–5

risk management 245–6
runners 41, 43

safety review board 213–14
sales
    break-even analysis 196
    business development
        and 25–31
    financial reporting 258
    forecasting 176–9
    overheads 261
    selling techniques 191–2
    tactical sales techniques 186
sales action processes 190–1
sales-force 186, 193–6
    control systems 194
    effectiveness 193
    evaluation and appraisal 194–5
    measures of performance 195–6
    time allocation 194–5
sales planning 188–90
    account classification 188–9
    business plan 25–6
    price sensitivity and matrix
        pricing 190
    territorial structure 189
sales and profit variance
    analysis 53–4
sanctions
    capital 272–4
    investment 269–71
savings 274
schedules 74–5
    adherence to 266
    master production schedule 43,
        156
segmentation, market *see* market
    segments
selling techniques 191–2
Shainin, Peter 217, 218
sign-off review 131–4
simultaneous engineering 107
site-location strategy 39, 40

skills requirement 75
Smith, Adam 3
space, factory 141–5
specification 74
  technical 78–9, 272–3
SPIN technique 192
spreadsheets 20
staff support activities 5, 46–7, 276
stakeholders 228, 229
standard industrial classification
  (SIC) code 176, 181
statistical process control
  charts 218
statistical process control
  methods 216–18
STEP 20
stock 266
  analysis of stocks 54, 261
  inventory control 156
strangers 41, 43
strategic agenda 185–6
strategic analysis 171–2
strategic local market
  planning 180–1
strategic sourcing 140–1, 142–3
strategy development 11–15, 55–6
strengths 55, 183
structure: organisation 4–6, 7, 43,
  56–7
supplier performance 266
suppliers 228
supplies module team 141
supply-chain management 4,
  137–68
  aspects and manufacturing
    policy 43
  assembly and test activities 149,
    150–1
  business plan 36–44
  factory space and
    location 141–5
  human resources 162–5
  internal factory capacity 150–5
  ISO 9000 standard 215–16

machining facilities 149–50,
  152–4
manufacturing system and
  equipment 145–8
measures of performance 156–9
operational improvement 39–43
organisation 160–1
overview 139–40
present situation 39
product introduction
  process 166, 167
production planning and
  control 156, 157
quality systems 161–2, 163
strategic sourcing 140–1, 142–3
supply-chain manager 5, 11
SWOT (strengths, weaknesses,
  opportunities and threats)
  analysis 55, 183

tactical sales techniques 186
task matrix 237–8
team working 107–8
teams
  customer-focused 210
  improvement 127, 210
  project *see* project teams
technical appraisal 114, 117–18,
  121–2, 127–30, 133–4
technical change 245
technical and commercial
  reviews *see* review
  mechanisms
technical compliance 222–3
technical and cost
  evaluation 78–80
technical resources 36, 37
technical specification 78–9, 272–3
technology
  core technologies 32, 100
  product and process
    technology 74
technology route map 32–4,
  97–100

technology trends 29
terms and conditions 86
territorial structure 189
test: assembly and test
    activities 149, 150–1
threats 55, 183
time
    allocation of
        salesperson's 194–5
    control parameters 248
timing of product launch 81
trading profit 259
training 129, 223
    customer-focused
        programmes 208–11
    sales-force 193
trends
    key industry trends 29
    projected 26, 28
    technology trends 29

US Department of Defense 208
users 174, 175

validation: concept *see* concept
    validation
validation test results 122
value-added content 177, 178, 179
values 206–7
video-conferencing 20
vision 56
    creating and
        communicating 204–7

Warwick International
    Manufacturing Group 11
weaknesses 55, 183
winning the contract 90–2
word processing 20
working environment 6–9